the MANual

BROADWAY BOOKS

NEW YORK

HUNTER S. FULGHUM

the MAN*ual*

THE GUY'S GUIDE TO BEING A
MAN'S MAN

Broadway Books titles may be purchased for business or promotional use or for special sales. For information, please write to: Special Markets Department, Random House, Inc., 1745 Broadway, New York, NY 10019.

PRINTED IN THE UNITED STATES OF AMERICA

BROADWAY BOOKS and its logo, a letter B bisected on the diagonal, are trademarks of Random House, Inc.

Visit our webside at www.broadwaybooks.com

First edition published 2004

Library of Congress Cataloging-in-Publication Data

Fulghum, Hunter S. (Hunter Samuel)
    The man-ual : the guy's guide to being a man's man / Hunter Fulghum.—1st ed.
      p. cm.
    1. Men—Life skills guides.   2. Men—Life skills guides—Humor.   I. Title: Manual.   II. Title: Guy's guide to being a man's man.   III. Title.
HQ1090.F85 2004
646.7'0081—dc22

                     2003062769

ISBN 0-7679-1489-9

10 9 8 7 6 5 4 3 2 1

The dedication for this book is available to you, the reader.
You may write your own or chose from one of several catchy,
preapproved dedications. Simply fill in your name and cross out the ones
you aren't using. (Use one of those really heavy black markers.)

To _____, my best friend. I love ya, man.

To _____, the man who taught me the
meaning of life and friendship.

To _____, the man who saved my life during
that firefight at Basra. You're the finest friend a guy could
have. Semper fi, bro!

For a modest fee, your name can be dropped as a "major influence and
shaper of the book" during radio and television interviews. If you are
interested in this service, please contact me care of the publisher
to discuss terms.

Acknowledgments

For me, the favorite part of writing a book—not counting cashing the advance check and finishing the thing so I can have a life again—is right here, where I get to say thanks publicly.

As always, there are a fair number of people who need to be mentioned, and if I try to get all of you, I'll do one of those Academy Award I'm-rambling-because-my-brain-just-locked-up kind of speeches. I know I'm neglecting (and possibly offending) a few dozen people, but to make it up to you, if I ever make it onto the *New York Times* bestseller list, you and a guest are invited to the party (yes, it will be open bar).

Moving right along into the heart of the matter—Becky, thank you.

Contents

Introduction

Just as there are all kinds of guys—regular guys, good guys, bad guys, youse guys, guys 'n' dolls, and so on—there are all kinds of things a guy needs to know. This manual is intended to provide a good, solid (albeit selective) set of information for the average-man-at-the-wheel-of-the-Ford F150-pickup kind of guy, to help him be a more well-rounded and reliable guy.

This book recognizes that guy information comes in several varieties:

- Stuff guys are aware of, might encounter in their day-to-day life, but aren't really clear on—how a woman's bra size is determined, for example.
- Stuff that all guys should know if they are to feel comfortable in the company of other guys—the basics of hockey, the demolition derby, and NASCAR.
- Do-it-yourself stuff. Every guy needs to know how to do certain things, particularly how to do things that are largely in the guy domain. If your father was doing his job, he taught you about the order of hands in poker and how to light a cigar. If he didn't, then it's here for your self-improvement.
- Useless and unimportant facts, the kinds of things that Cliff

from *Cheers* might have shared with his buddies in the bar. Guys are masters of the useless fact, stat, or detail. And I have gone way out of my way to find interesting and trivial facts you won't find assembled anywhere else. (Notably absent are the reams and reams of sports trivia factoids and stats, which are painfully detailed in other books, and frankly, are tedious to read anyway. If you want those, you'll find them elsewhere.)

ALCOHOL

A lot of people want you to think about returning to the lifestyles of simpler cultures—like the precontact American Indians. These people see this as a more natural, touchy-feely, one with the environment, live in harmony with the land, nuts and berries, treat your body as a temple way to be. Pretty damned irritating people, all things considered.

Fact is, we got introduced to smoking courtesy of Native Americans (and every time I light up a good cigar, I offer a thanks to them). And alcohol? Probably some nomadic tribesman found a little honey that had fermented in the sun. Whatever the case, you can bet that the minute he got his first "beer buzz" going, he was on the lookout for honey bees.

All About Alcohol

MICROBIAL DUNG—FERMENTATION

The basic requirements to make alcohol are yeast, sugar, water, and heat. The proper mixture of these ingredients will cause yeast to consume the sugar and produce alcohol as a waste product—a sort of microbial dung—along with carbon dioxide, which gives fermentation its characteristic smell and also causes some natural carbonation.

Yeasts are fungi, and grow as single cells, budding off new growth or dividing into two separate cells. Like other fungi, their spores are light and are transported readily in the air, allowing easy spread. It is believed that the first human experiences with yeast in bread, for example, probably occurred when natural yeast landed in bread dough, causing it to rise and become fluffier.

The most commonly used strain of yeast is *Saccharomyces cerevisiae,* which is used in the fermentation of many grains to produce alcohol, as well as in baking. This strain is most commonly called baker's yeast or brewer's yeast. *Saccharomyces carlsbergensis* is another common yeast, used heavily in the production of beers, while *Saccharomyces cerevisiae* is used for ales.

- "Malted milk" is made by combining dried milk and malted grain.
- Seven percent of the Irish barley crop goes toward making Guinness beer.

The sugar necessary for fermentation is provided by grains, cereals, or fruits, though other sources may be used. When brewers use grains, they "malt" them, steeping them in water to force germination, which causes the seeds to begin converting starches to sugar. The starches are part of the seed and normally feed the plant embryo, in much the same way an egg yolk feeds the embryonic chicken. (Note: Attempting to make alcohol by fermenting chicken eggs or chickens is not recommended.) Wine was originally fermented using the naturally occurring yeasts commonly found on the grapes in the vineyards. In modern production, sulfur dioxide is added to crushed grapes to kill naturally occurring yeasts and molds, allowing the vintner to introduce a preferred strain of yeast.

In addition to corn sugars, which are the most commonly used, other sources of sugar and flavor for alcohol include honey, cane sugar, rye, corn, rice, wheat, sorghum, bananas, melons, apples, peaches, pears, and tree sap.

ALL ABOUT BEER

"Beer" is the generic term for a low-alcohol-content beverage brewed from cereal grains, malt, and hops. What Americans call beer is what the British consider "lager." Lagers are made with bottom-brewing yeasts, and are best served at 38°F. Ales, which are an older style of beer, are made with top-brewing yeasts, best served at 50°F, and include stouts, porters, and wheat beers.

Prior to 1800, most beer was ale. The lager method of brewing was introduced in Germany, marking the beginning of the modern era for beer, which is dominated by lagers.

The first historical evidence of beer was found at an archeological site in the lower river valleys of what was once called Mesopotamia (now Iran and Iraq). At the ruin of the Sumerian city Godin Tepe, a pottery vessel with a crisscross of grooves was unearthed by archeologists. The grooves contained traces of a pale yellow compound identified as calcium oxalate, a principal component of beer. Archeologists suggest that the grooves were used to catch sediment in the beer. The site dates back to the middle of the fourth millennium B.C. Evidence has also been found to suggest that the Sumerians were making wine at about the same time. Babylonian records from this era found on clay tablets include recipes for beer making, and beer was so highly valued that it was often used as part of the payment given workers.

Beer was known in ancient Egypt (possibly as a result of trade with Mesopotamia). It was associated with the Egyptian gods Neprit and

Osiris, and both beer and bread were important in the afterlife where, ancient Egyptian stories tell, bread never decays and beer never grows stale.

Julius Caesar is credited with introducing beer making to northern Europe during the conquest of Gaul (France), which may have led to brewing in northern Europe in general. After the fall of the Roman Empire and the beginning of the Middle Ages (A.D. 500 to A.D. 1500), the tradition of beer making continued, largely in monasteries. Hops, which add the flavor distinct to modern European- and American-style beers, were introduced into European brewing around the end of the Middle Ages.

BEER SAINTS

After Saint Patrick, one of the most well-known Irish saints is Brigid (also known as the "Mary of the Gael"). She lived between A.D. 457 and 525 and founded the monastery of Kildare. Saint Brigid was well regarded for her spirituality, charity, and compassion. She was also fond of beer. A popular story about Brigid tells how she was working in a leper colony which found itself without beer. When the lepers she nursed asked her for beer, and there was none, she changed the bath water into an excellent beer by the sheer strength of her blessing and dealt it out to the thirsty. Brigid is reported to have changed her dirty bathwater to beer for the benefit of visiting clerics.

Saint Arnold of Metz said, "Don't drink the water, drink beer." It appears he was concerned with the health risks of drinking impure water, and understood that the water used in the production of beer, which involved boiling, was safer. According to legend, he stopped a plague by placing his crucifix in a brew kettle and telling people to drink only from this "blessed" vessel. He is also credited with saying, "From man's sweat and God's love, beer came into the world."

CULTURED TOASTS

The classic American drinking salutation is "Cheers," which reflects the prominence of English culture in the United States (even though more of us have German heritage than English). The well-educated traveler should have a ready knowledge of local toasts, such as:

Albanian: *Gezur!*

Finnish: *Kippis!*

Chinese: *Ganbei!* Literal translation is "Dry glass."

French: *A votre santé!* Pronounced "Ah vote-reh sant-eh." Literal translation is "To your health."

German: *Prosit!* Pronounced "Pro-st."

Greek: *Yasas!*

Hebrew: *L'chayim!* Pronounced "Lah-heim." Literal translation is "To life."

Hungarian: *Kedves egeszegere!*

Irish: *Slainte!* Pronounced "Slan-cher." Literal translation is "To your health."

Italian: *Alla salute!*

Japanese: *Kempai!* Pronounced "Kem-pie."

Polish: *Na zdrowie!* Pronounced "Na stroviya." Literal translation is "To your health."

Russian: *Na zdorovye!* Pronounced similarly to the Polish expression. Also means "To your health."

Spanish: *Salud!* Pronounced "Sah-lood." Literal translation is "Health."

Swahili: *Furah!* Pronounced "Foo-RAH."

Swedish: *Skal!* Pronounced "Skol."

Zulu: *Poo zim pee la!*

(Author's note: Yeah, we don't have all the translations or pronunciations. First off, it is really hard to find a reliable resource for a toast in Zulu, much less explain what it means or how to say it. Second, they all—generally—mean "Wahoo, we're drinking!" And finally, like you know any Hungarians who're gonna call you on how you say *Kedves egeszegere?* 'Nuf said on that . . .)

BEER GLASSES (NOT TO BE CONFUSED WITH "BEER GOGGLES")

Beer can be imbibed directly from any handy container, however, beer aficionados maintain that the proper glass should be used, depending on the type of beer. The shape and style of glass should be matched to the character of the beer to enhance and reinforce flavor and drinking experience. Examples are:

- In October of 1880, the Cincinnati Red Stockings (later the "Reds") were expelled from the National League for serving beer at their ball park. They were returned to the league in 1890.
- Noah's provisions on the Ark included beer.

Goblets: wide with a stemmed base. Goblets prevent a runaway head, and are used with frutier beers.

Flutes: tall and thin, and should be used with pilsners. The drinker should pour to adjust the head height to the individual's taste.

Mugs (such as steins): short and wide. These are preferred for strong beers, allowing a taller head.

TULIPS: shaped like the flower on a tulip, and are best for stronger beers. They tend to cause a taller head in many beers.

SNIFTERS: wider toward the bottom and narrow at the top. These accentuate aromatic beers by concentrating the smells.

BRITISH PINT: tapering from wide at the top to narrow at the bottom, these are a tradition in pubs, selected largely for function (they stack well and are robust). They do moderately well at concentrating smells.

When in doubt, drink from the can or bottle. Who can keep track of all these shapes anyway?

- The reason that German beer steins have lids dates back several hundred years. The lids were intended to keep flies and filth out of the beer, which was more of a problem then than now. The reason for the glass bottoms found in some steins is not clear.

- Beer cans were introduced in 1935 by the American Can Company and Kreuger Brewing.

SAFER BEER GLASSES

In 1998 the English Labor Party proposed banning traditional beer glasses in pubs. The motivation behind the legislation arose from concern over drunks or troublemakers smashing the glasses commonly used in pubs (the traditional English pint) and using the jagged edges as weapons. The legislation would have required a toughened safety glass to be substituted for the bar glass. The proposal was discarded when it was revealed that after repeated exposure to heat from washing, the safety glass could be easily smashed into very wicked shards.

The Down Side

HANGOVER CAUSES

Sunday morning. Your tongue is glued to the roof of your mouth and you woke up next to the toilet (again). Dude! You're hung over!

Though it isn't universally viewed as such, alcohol is a drug and it alters your body chemistry. One of the primary effects is to reduce the sugar production of amino acids in the liver. All cells need sugar to survive, and a lack of it slows brain activity and impairs physical function in general. Alcohol also forces the liver to work harder to remove chemicals known as "congeners," mildly toxic compounds produced during fermentation. It typically takes the liver one hour to process one drink's worth of congeners from the body.

Alcohol is a diuretic. As alcohol is introduced into the body, the kidneys work harder to eliminate the alcohol, which causes dehydration. Traditional wisdom has always suggested that drinking black coffee is a good remedy for a hangover. This is not true. While the caffeine in regular coffee may give a temporary energy boost, it is also a diuretic and will worsen the dehydration.

Drinking places stresses on

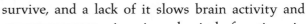
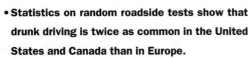

- Statistics on random roadside tests show that drunk driving is twice as common in the United States and Canada than in Europe.
- When a person drinks alcohol, it will show up in a Breathalyzer. This is because the body absorbs the alcohol from the mouth, throat, stomach, and intestines into the bloodstream. Alcohol is not digested or chemically changed in the bloodstream. As the alcohol-laden blood passes through the lungs, some of the alcohol moves across the membranes of the lung's air sacs (the alveoli) and into the exhaled air. The concentration of the alcohol in the air can be measured and quantified to determine the concentration of the alcohol in the blood.
- Of those countries with available data, Mauritania has the lowest consumption of alcohol per person, at 0.02 liters per year. France is reported to have the highest rate of consumption, at 20.28 liters per person per year.

the body that have a varying effect, depending on the physical condition of the drinker in general and at the time of drinking. Being tired, sick, or in poor condition is likely to cause a significantly worse hangover. "Condition" as a drinker also contributes. A regular exposure to alcohol can actually reduce hangovers (though there are other serious effects resulting from overuse of alcohol). A drinker used to moderate intake who engages in a heavy round of drinking is likely to experience a worse hangover than a heavy drinker.

Alcohol is a depressant, and heavy drinking is essentially a spike of exposure to the drug with all the related effects. The end of a binge and the purging of the alcohol by the body can result in a state of nervous hypersensitivity, which increases the discomfort of headache, muscle pain, and other physical side effects.

Finally, the severity of a hangover depends on both the quantity of alcohol as well as the type. Some alcohol contains a higher percentage of congeners, which are serious hangover inducers. Generally, the darker the drink, the more congeners. Vodka, for example, has very little whereas bourbon has the highest levels and causes serious hangovers.

HANGOVER PREVENTION AND REMEDIES

The only proven way to prevent a hangover is to not drink. There are no "magic bullets," but there are ways to minimize the pain and quicken the speed of recovery:

Before You Drink
- Eat oily food or drink whole milk before drinking. In theory, the fat slows the absorption of alcohol and lets the body eliminate it before experiencing the worst of it. Eating starchy foods is recommended as well.
- Drink plenty of water. This helps to counteract the diuretic properties of alcohol.

While You Drink

- Do not mix different kinds of alcohol.
- Do not overindulge in alcohol that is heavily colored—cordials, dark rum, etc.
- Avoid red wines and alcohol with lots of additives, such as brandy or sherry.
- Stick to vodka or white wine.

When It's Too Late

- Drink plenty of water.
- Take vitamins (C in particular).
- Get some exercise. This helps to metabolize the excess alcohol out of the system.
- Eat foods high in fructose.
- Hair of the dog. A small quantity of alcohol taken the morning after will frequently lessen the pain, though only temporarily.
- Take analgesics, antacids, and other treatments for headache and nausea after drinking.
- Take a hot bath, sauna, or steam bath to help sweat the toxins out of your system. (Note: My editor wonders if this is safe and if you might die and then your heirs will sue her, me, and the publishing house. I see this is a real concern and I want to go on record as advising you not to take a bath, sauna, or steam bath ever again.)

(Note: If you are a guy with long hair, we recommend you pull it back before you start drinking heavily. Nothing worse than puking in your own hair.)

DRIVING UNDER THE INFLUENCE

Laws in the United States regarding operating a vehicle while under the influence or even partaking of alcohol in a vehicle have become significantly more restrictive in the past few years. Punishments vary in this country depending on jurisdiction and past arrests, but generally begin with the loss of driving privileges and can lead to fines and jail time. Overseas, the punitive measures taken are similarly straightforward in some countries, and very creative and even weird in others.

In Norway, for example, the first offense will cost three weeks in jail at hard labor, whereas in Finland and Sweden the punishment is jail for a year at hard labor. A second offense in Norway within five years means loss of driving privileges for life. In the United Kingdom, it's a $250 fine, suspension for a year, and a year in jail, whereas the French will quadruple the fine and triple the suspension, but jail time is limited to one year. In South Africa, a DUI can cost jail for ten years, a fine of $10,000, or both. The Russians will take the offender's license away for life.

In Australia, by contrast, a drunk driver will have his name printed up in the local newspapers under the heading "He's Drunk and in Jail." (One assumes that the driver in question will be in jail.)

The Malaysians and Turks show the range of divergent punishments. In Malaysia, a DUI means jail time for the drinker *and* his or her spouse. The Turks take a gentler view: an intoxicated driver will be taken for a ride out of town and then forced to walk back under police escort, essentially long enough for the driver to sober up.

Finally, the governments of Bulgaria and El Salvador exercise the most extreme punishments, the firing squad. In Bulgaria, at least, the execution comes only after the second offense.

See also "Crime, Punishment, and the Police," page 147.

WOMEN, SEX, AND GETTING NAKED

Women are without doubt the greatest mystery a guy faces. They have things we are fascinated by (breasts, for example), and yet we do not fully understand so much of their world. Equally, they do not understand us, so don't let them read this book; that would lead to an unfair advantage. But if knowledge is power, this chapter may just give you a bit of an edge. At least you'll know when she's lying about her cup size . . .

Breasts and the Things That Cover Them

THE BIKINI

Two-piece bathing suits were not an entirely new concept when the bikini was introduced in 1946. In 1943, during the Second World War, the United States government mandated a 10 percent reduction in the use of fabric in women's swimwear. Several manufacturers eliminated the midriff section of their suits and the skirt panels that covered the hips and bottom to comply. While these were technically two-piece suits like the bikini, they were very conservative by contrast (and were much more acceptable, being a patriotic show of support for the war effort as opposed to an attempt to pander to our baser instincts).

Louis Reard, a French clothing designer, introduced the "bikini" on July 5, 1946, four days after the first U.S. atomic bomb test on Bikini Atoll. Jaques Heim, another French designer, had introduced a similar design (the "atome") just before this, calling it the world's smallest bathing suit, so Reard billed his as "smaller than the world's smallest bathing suit."

The bikini and atome designs were both two-piece suit designs made with a minimal amount of fabric, revealing a whole lot of bare skin. When Reard tried to show the suit, no respectable model would wear it. Eventually he hired Micheline Bernardini, a nude dancer from the Casino de Paris, as the model.

The bikini was banned on many beaches, deemed low class and the attire of prostitutes, but women, Europeans in particular, warmed to it. In 1955 pinup girl Diana Dors wore a mink bikini to the Venice Film Festival, and in 1957 French actress Brigitte Bardot appeared in a bikini in *And God Created Woman.* Both helped to make the public more comfortable with the suit.

• **Even though she appeared in several bikini beach-party movies, Annette Funicello never wore a bikini on screen.**

In 1960 the release of the song "Itsy Bitsy Teeny Weeny Yellow Polka Dot Bikini" spurred a serious wave of bikini buying in the United States. Two years later, the release of the first James Bond film, *Dr. No,* brought the suit into view to a worldwide audience, further enhancing its popularity. Scandinavian actress Ursula Andress appeared in a bikini (though a very modest one by modern standards) in the film, raising a few eyebrows but encouraging Americans to reconsider the suit style. In the mid-sixties, the bikini beach-party movies hit the scene with all-American kids Annette Funicello and Frankie Avalon, positioning the suit in a wholesome light.

The trend toward more skin and less fabric—obviously in the interests of conservation—led to both the monokini (think nothing more than a pair of panties) and the thong. Alas, the monokini never caught on, but thankfully the thong did.

MEASUREMENT OF CUP SIZE

Bra sizes are given in two parts: the circumference and cup size. The circumference is the measure around and is given in inches, whereas the cup size is the measure of the volume of the individual breast, and is assigned a letter designator. A typical bra size might be expressed as a 32B or a 44DD. (Note: Wear eye protection when confronted with anything D and above.) Determining these sizes is done as follows:

1. The initial measurement is taken in inches under the breasts with a cloth tape measure pulled completely around the woman's torso and back to the starting place. The tape should not be pulled tight, but should be snug and accurately follow the natural curve of the body. Read the number from the tape, add five inches, rounding up to the nearest even number. Record this result as "A."

2. The second measurement is taken at the fullest part of her bosom—typically this will be at the nipples. Again, the tape should be wrapped completely around the chest and should not be pulled tight. Record this number as "B."

3. To determine cup size, "A" is subtracted from "B." This result is compared against the following table:

B minus A (inches)	Cup Size
0	AA
1	A
2	B
3	C
4	D
5	DD/E
6	F
7	G

It should be noted that this method and table are not universally accepted or consistently applied by all manufacturers. It is a rule of thumb used by the fitters of ladies' bras, and variations on the formula for obtaining cup size exist, though the general approach is the same.

CUPS

It is true that it is what is in the bra that counts. But here's what you might encounter on your way in:

Full Cup: Full cup refers to the coverage of the breast by the bra's cups—usually completely covering the breast—and is chosen most often for modesty and structural support.

Demi-cup: A demi-cup covers only the lower portion of the breast, extending just above the nipple. Demi cups are intended to show more cleavage, and are frequently designed to push the breasts forward and toward the centerline of the chest.

Baseball Cup: The distinguishing characteristic of the baseball cup is the seam on the cup, which runs horizontally across the nipple line of the cup, curving as it does so. The effect it produces is similar to the seam on a baseball. (Remember, just as with a good curve ball, finger placement is key with the baseball cup.)

Contour Cup Bra: A contour cup is lightly padded with a soft cup, and is usually intended for C size cups and smaller.

Underwire: The underwire in a bra is a metal or plastic support sewn into the lower curve of the bra cups to offer greater support. Underwire bras may have individual wires in each cup, or a continuous wire that links both cups together.

Scoop Front: A scoop-front bra is cut low in the front, exposing a great deal of the breasts and cleavage.

Push-up Bra: A push-up bra is designed to enhance the breast, using sewn in or removable pads. The pads are usually located at the side and bottom of each cup, causing the breasts to be thrust forward and up.

Sports Bra: The sports bra is a soft, one-piece bra, intended for wear during exercise or sporting events. The bras are designed to minimize chafing and discomfort. They come off really easily too.

See also "Women's Undergarments."

WOMEN'S UNDERGARMENTS

Men have boxers, briefs, or we go commando. It's just not that simple for women:

PANTIES AND BRA: The basic modern undergarment, the panty and bra set comes in a variety of sizes, shapes, and styles, though the basic configuration is a pair of snug shorts worn at the lower torso and a fabric sling to support the breasts. Bras vary depending on the type of outfit worn, the size of the breasts in question, and the effect desired. See "Measurement of Cup Size" and sidebar "Cups" for additional information.

TEDDIES: A teddy is a one-piece undergarment, combining a loose bra and panties more like boxers than panties. Teddies provide less support to the bosom and should never be worn by women with breasts larger than 34C. It's just *wrong*.

GARTER BELTS: Garter belts predate panty hose and are uncommon in contemporary times. They consist of a lightweight belt worn around the waist, with elastic straps at the front and back of each leg. Stockings are clipped to the straps to hold the hose up and keep them snug and smooth. Stockings may be nylon, though silk is more traditional. Your grandma wore these . . . sorry, bad image.

CORSETS: Corsets are archaic items, no longer worn by most women, though they have a loyal following among fans of certain styles of dress and sexual recreations. They were largely used for slimming the figure and consisted of cloth laced up around the midriff, below the breasts and above the hips. Tightening the laces pulled the waist in and accentuated the hips and bosom. Tightening them too much caused internal injuries. Your great-grandmother probably wore one, but so does Lady Fiona from the House of Leather.

- The cotton T-shirt was introduced to America by GIs returning from Europe at the end of World War One. European soldiers wore a lightweight cotton undershirt instead of the wool ones provided by the U.S. military. U.S. soldiers adopted them for comfort.
- An adult novelty shop in Houston, Texas, was stopped from selling a line of edible underwear, because city authorities said it did not have the proper food service license to do so.

ALL-IN-ONE: The modern version of the corset, an all-in-one serves a similar purpose in slimming the figure, but more closely resembles a one-piece bathing suit, combining panties and bra in one continuous item.

BUSTIERS: A bustier is like a cross between a bra and a corset. It has a low band that passes below the breasts and lifts them, cupping only the lower portion of the breast. It is favored by women when they wear strapless gowns.

GIRDLES: A girdle is similar to the corset as an item of apparel for slimming, though it typically covers the area between the waist and the mid-thigh, and includes panties. Your mother wore a girdle.

THONGS: Thongs are a variation on panties, though much sheerer and cut higher on the hips. Thongs are often worn to minimize the lines produced under clothing by larger, more traditional panties. Also known as "butt floss."

EDIBLE UNDERWEAR

Edible underwear was invented in 1976 by Cosmerotica, a Chicago-based novelty company. The underwear is manufactured from a material not unlike fruit leather, but with fewer vitamins and a higher sugar content. Since their original introduction they've been made available both in men's briefs and women's panties, and as bras and condoms. The flavor range includes cherry, grape, chocolate, passion fruit, and banana. Edible underwear melts in water, and will gum up the filter in the spa or pool faster than your girlfriend's hair gel.

Nudity and Getting Naked

NUDITY LAWS

Nudity and the Law is a complex combination, depending on location, circumstances, cultural and social perceptions, religious views, and property rights. It is generally accepted that nudity within a private residence is of no concern to the public or the judicial systems, though in Singapore nudity within the home is illegal.

Western cultures formerly classified public nudity as "indecent exposure"; however, the distinction is often made between simple nudity and nudity with intent to offend or commit malicious or sexual acts. The logic of a nude beach is that the only people who should be there are those who are not offended by nudity.

Some interpretations of nudity are related to the primary sexual organs. Specifically, if the genitals are exposed in a public environment, legal action may be pursued. A pair of women successfully defended themselves in court against a charge of indecent exposure (for jogging in the nude) by arguing that the primary sexual organs of women are not easily visible (being largely internal) and therefore no indecent exposure occurred. One assumes that they didn't happen to run past or over anyone who was lying down.

In spite of the slow change in attitude about nudity, there are still many cultures that enforce strict legal standards against nudity. A few examples of actual laws:

- **When several milk-producing glands feed to a fleshy protuberance separately, this is called a nipple. When milk glands feed into a common reservoir that then feeds into a protuberance, the proper term is a "teat." Humans and primates have nipples. Cows have teats.**
- **Women's areolas (the area around the nipple) tend to darken and enlarge during pregnancy. Part of the reason for this is that new babies are highly responsive to contrasting colors and the darker areola stands out more against the lighter tone of the breast. In simpler terms, a darker, larger nipple makes a better target.**

- In England it is illegal for boys under the age of ten to see a naked mannequin.
- In Thailand you must wear underwear when you are away from home.
- In Minnesota it is illegal to sleep in the nude.
- In Oklahoma women may not gamble in the nude or while wearing only lingerie or a towel.

THE GREATEST NUDE BEACHES

Remember, it is considered rude to stare at people at a nude beach. Especially if they're two-bagger ugly.

Samurai Beach, Australia: Home of the annual Nude Olympics. An event not to be missed.

Montelivet, France: Found on the Atlantic coast of France, this beach is safe and nudism is completely legal.

Wreck Beach, British Columbia, Canada: The water is cold even on the sunniest of summer days, but the scenery is incredible. Be prepared for a lot of pale skin, though—this is Canada after all.

Red White and Blue Beach, California: The beach and adjacent area are privately owned, so that visitors can be naked pretty much anywhere.

Little Beach, Maui, Hawaii: Isolated and perfect for a little naturism. Nudism is illegal in Hawaii, but the laws are generally not enforced at Little Beach.

Red Beach, Crete, Greece: Nudity is allowed anywhere at the beach or the adjacent resort except the dining room.

NIPPLES

Mammals all have mammary glands to produce milk for their young. Some scientists believe they evolved from sweat glands, though no immediate explanation for this is offered. These modified glands surface on the exterior of the body in the form of nipples or teats.

The location and number of nipples or teats varies widely, usually in proportion to the size of the animal's litters. One species of rat found in Africa has so many young that the females have nipples arranged from under their forelimbs to the middle of their thighs. Humans and primates are in the minority with one pair of nipples arranged symmetrically on either side of the pectoral area.

Sex and Attraction

COMMON ABBREVIATIONS IN PERSONAL ADS

Abbreviations in personal advertisements that are used as a means of finding a mate started out in newspapers, where the cost was related to the length of the ad. (Please note, no one ever felt a need to develop an abbreviation for "butt-ugly.") In the Internet era, electronic personal ads have maintained this shorthand, expanding it to reflect the greater diversity of the population (and their interests). For first-timers, here's a good cross-section of the stuff you'll encounter.

A: Asian—covers a broad range, but is usually in reference to people from Japan, Korea, China, and Vietnam

B: Black

BBW: Big Beautiful Woman—a euphemism. Hope you like 'em a bit on the chunky side.

B&D: Bondage and Discipline

BDSM: Bondage/Discipline/Sadism/Masochism

C: Christian

D: Divorced

D&S: Dominance and Submission

DP: Disabled Person

F: Female

G: Gay/Lesbian

H: Hispanic

HPW: Height and Weight Proportional—see "BBW" above

ISO: In Search Of

J: Jewish

L: Lesbian

LBD: Light Bondage and Discipline

LD: Light Drinker

LS: Light Smoker

LJBF: Let's Just Be Friends—means do not assume you'll be having sex with this person.

LTR: Long-Term Relationship

M: Male/Married—judge by context

NA: Native American

NCaH: No Children at Home

ND: No Drugs

NS: Non-Smoker

NSTDs: No Sexually Transmitted Diseases

P: Petite/Professional—judge by context

S: Single

SOH: Sense of Humor

S&M, S/M: Sadism and Masochism or Sadomasochism

SO: Significant Other

W: White

WLTM: Would Like To Meet

NAMES FOR UNUSUAL SEXUAL BEHAVIORS

The range of technical and nontechnical terms for sexual behaviors and interests includes many which were not commonly understood as recently as ten years ago. Changes in society, media, and values have opened up the recognition (if not acceptance) of these across a wider segment of the population; however, there are many more behaviors that are not as commonly known, or names for common behaviors that are not commonly used. The following are a few examples.

Amomaxia: Sex in a parked car (which is much safer than sex in a moving car, especially with a manual transmission).

Gendoloma: Fantasizing during sex to hasten orgasm.

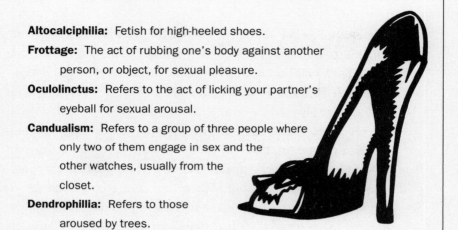

Altocalciphilia: Fetish for high-heeled shoes.

Frottage: The act of rubbing one's body against another person, or object, for sexual pleasure.

Oculolinctus: Refers to the act of licking your partner's eyeball for sexual arousal.

Candualism: Refers to a group of three people where only two of them engage in sex and the other watches, usually from the closet.

Dendrophillia: Refers to those aroused by trees.

APHRODISIACS

An aphrodisiac is a substance, including food, drinks, drugs, or scents that will increase sexual performance and desire or arouse the sexual interest of the person ingesting or exposed to the aphrodisiac. The name in English is derived from the ancient Greek goddess of love, Aphrodite, and the list of items that are considered to have aphrodisiac characteristics is exceedingly long and varied.

Aphrodisiacs can be broken down into three basic categories:

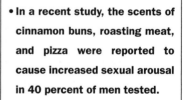

• In a recent study, the scents of cinnamon buns, roasting meat, and pizza were reported to cause increased sexual arousal in 40 percent of men tested.

1. Similarity. When the aphrodisiac bears a strong resemblance to sexual organs, it is considered to fall under the category of "similarity." The user associates the similarity to a sex organ with a benefit in the form of added energy, sexual prowess, or increased pleasure.

Ginseng is an example. The name translates literally as "man's root," and the root of the plant often looks like the penis (sort of). Taking it on a regular regimen is considered to improve stamina, as well as overall health. Rhino horn and oysters are also in this group, rhino horn for the similarity to an erect penis, and the oyster for similarity to the vagina—though the resemblance in the latter case is not an attractive one and to make the comparison does an injustice to the vagina.

2. Reputation for Procreation. The products of animals that have reputations for virility, frequent and impressive sexual performance, or simply seem to be powerful sexually because of their other characteristics, are believed to imbue one with added energy or attraction. Typically aphrodisiacs use the genitals or reproductive organs, and they include penis of rabbit, goat, and tiger.

3. Sexual Symptoms. Foods and chemicals that induce physical symptoms similar to those felt during sex, such as sweating and elevated heart rate, are said to be aphrodisiacs. Hot peppers, curries, and other spicy foods are all examples. One of the more famous is Spanish fly. (See sidebar "Spanish Fly.")

SPANISH FLY

Spanish fly is not Spanish nor is it a fly. It is made from a beetle, specifically emerald-green blister beetles, *Cantharis vesicatoria* or *Lytta vesicatoria*. The beetles are dried and crushed, and the resulting powder acts as both an irritant and a diuretic when ingested. The irritant factor is believed to be the primary reason for associating the compound with sex and arousal. Spanish fly was mentioned in written histories and commentaries by Hippocrates and Pliny, and was reportedly given by the Roman empress Livia to other members of the royal family in the hope of making them commit sexual indiscretions that could later be used against them.

Other aphrodisiacs include:

Tiger penis: Rubbed on the phallus for improved performance.

Asparagus: Plant shape is suggestive of the penis. Asparagus can be woody, and so can . . .

Betel nut: The nut of the betel palm is not only reported to work as an aphrodisiac, but also to expel wind, kill germs, and act as a deodorant when eaten.

Chocolate: Chocolate was considered an aphrodisiac because of its rarity, though in more recent years medical science has suggested that there are chemicals in chocolate that stimulate the brain's pleasure centers and may have some benefit in bedding the opposite sex.

Avocados: The root of this word means "testicles" in Spanish.

Pearls dissolved in vinegar: Queen Cleopatra is reported to have been very fond of this, and it may have contributed to her sexual conquest of the Roman invaders of Egypt.

Green M&Ms: The power of the green M&M as an aphrodisiac qualifies as an urban legend. Still, an informal poll of college students found that more than 50 percent believe that the green ones do heighten sexual arousal. That explains the candy dish at the sorority house.

Coco-de-mer: Often called the "double coconut," these are actually the fruit of the *Lodoicea maldivica* tree and can reach up to forty pounds in weight. When whole, the fruit looks much like the lower part of a woman's torso, from mid-thigh to mid-belly, including the shape of the vulva. (If a woman really looks like the coco-de-mer, she's a bit on the hefty side.)

CONDOMS

A condom is a sheath worn over the penis to prevent pregnancy or the transmission of disease. Some say the term comes from the name of a physician who supplied them to a king of England, but the likely source is the Latin word *condon,* meaning a receptacle. Condoms that date back to 1640 have been found at Dudley Castle in England, but the oldest evidence of the use of the condom is found in Egyptian art, dating back to around 1000 B.C.

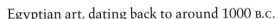

Condoms were initially made of natural materials, including linen or oiled silk, sheep intestine, and the flotation bladders of fish, and were tied on with string or ribbon—kind of like a present, except you don't want to unwrap this one during the party. Rubber condoms came into use in 1844 after the invention of vulcanized rubber. In spite of the availability of condoms due to mass production, there was significant public and societal pressure against their use. U.S. soldiers fighting in Europe in World War I were the only combatants denied the use of condoms, resulting in the American Expeditionary Force having the highest rate of sexually transmitted diseases of all involved armies.

- **During World War II, condoms were frequently used to cover the barrel of rifles carried ashore by amphibious assault troops to keep salt water from entering and corroding the inside of the rifle.**
- **Flavored condoms are available in England, and include such tasty delights as curry and scotch.**

A female condom is available. It consists of a loose rubber sheath that is placed inside the vagina. The end at the inside is closed by a ring (which also serves to hold it in place), while the other end is held open by a second ring. This second ring remains outside the vagina and partly covers the surrounding skin area.

DEFINITION OF GETTING TO A BASE

- First base is kissing, including open-mouth kissing (formally known as "French kissing," it has been renamed "liberty kissing" as a protest against the French refusal to support the United States in the Second Iraq War).

- Second base may include first base and adds touching, feeling, or fondling above the waist, most often the chest, breasts, and nipples. Definitions as to whether this is over or under clothing depends on regional and cultural interpretation.

- Third base may include first and/or second base, and allows touching and fondling below the waist, typically including the genitals and buttocks. At this stage, generally the hands are allowed under the clothing or the clothing is removed.

- Reaching home base or "hitting a home run" is full intercourse. Please note, it is not essential to get to first, second, or third before you hit a home run, but she'd probably like you to at least touch the bases on the way around.

- Oral sex without intercourse is not classified as any particular base, but would probably be an inside-the-park home run.

RACING, SPORTS, AND GAMES

Listen, sports *are* a fact of guy life. And for some guys, it just comes natural to know all the stats, the great players, and the moments that epitomize whatever game it is you happen to be talking about. On the other hand, it is *painful* to have to learn all that stuff, and most women find the endless recitation of Cal Ripken's lifetime statistics to be a total turnoff.

Compromise time. Learn the basics of sports, enough to sound reasonably well informed, and you can hold your own during guy quality time. And if the girls are around, impress them with a little of the lighter, "human" face of sports.

Fast Freaking Cars

NASCAR

NASCAR, short for National Association of Stock Car Auto Racing, was founded as a formal entity in 1948, though "stock" car racing—

competitions between drivers in cars in their original, off-the-lot condition—predates the creation of NASCAR by almost as many years as there have been cars.

NASCAR's president, Bill France Sr., 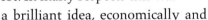 hit on the idea of racing regular cars—the "stock" cars that were available off the dealer's lot. In many respects this was a brilliant idea, economically and 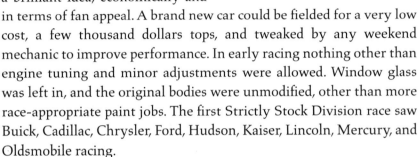 in terms of fan appeal. A brand new car could be fielded for a very low cost, a few thousand dollars tops, and tweaked by any weekend mechanic to improve performance. In early racing nothing other than engine tuning and minor adjustments were allowed. Window glass was left in, and the original bodies were unmodified, other than more race-appropriate paint jobs. The first Strictly Stock Division race saw Buick, Cadillac, Chrysler, Ford, Hudson, Kaiser, Lincoln, Mercury, and Oldsmobile racing.

As the racing began to get more serious, an inherent flaw in fielding a stock automobile was revealed: the pressures and wear of racing were more than unmodified, off-the-lot cars could handle. Failure of tires, wheels, and suspension were common, putting drivers at risk. (One grand champion, Tim Flock, installed a trapdoor in the floorboards of his car to allow him to check the wear on the right front tire—a particularly common point of failure.)

To address this, NASCAR began to allow modifications and improvements in the interests of safety, which eroded the "stock" nature of the cars, but decreased the frequency of accidents and injury. Car makers helped by producing cars with higher performance parts, making them stock since they were manufactured this way. The result was higher speeds and more exciting racing, and the manufacturers were provided with a test ground for new ideas and machinery.

In 1953 Lincoln, Hudson, and Oldsmobile all introduced severe usage kits for their stock cars, upgrading the suspension, axles, hubs, and spindles. Hudson also brought a twin-H carburetor to their cars, which allowed their cars to win twenty-two of thirty-seven races in 1953.

Chevy set the standard for power in stock cars when they introduced the V-8 355-cubic-inch engine which, with minor changes, is still a standard for GMC racing teams today. It is one of the most powerful engines ever built and mass produced for cars other than specialty models.

Since those early days, the sport has seen the introduction of aluminum brake drums, X-frame body design, and hemispherical combustion chamber engines (the famous "hemi"), among others. The modern NASCAR race car, with custom-built body, adjustable suspension, roll cage, spoiler, and other improvements bears little resemblance to the family car, though the improvements introduced for racing have directly benefited the cars driven by average people, including greater protection for drivers, better steering and braking systems, and improved tire and engine design.

NASCAR has thirteen different divisions, but the most celebrated is the Winston Cup Series, which features cars with up to 750-horsepower engines, capable of reaching 200 mph and above. The series includes thirty-six races on twenty-three different tracks around the country. The NASCAR Busch Series features cars lighter than the Winston Cup competitors, running with about 550-horsepower engines at lower

- **Roll cages (steel cages built around the driver's area to prevent him being crushed in an accident) were made a mandatory requirement in NASCAR in 1952. Tim Flock, who won the Modified Sportsman race at Daytona that year, was disqualified because his cage was made of wood.**
- **Two-way radios between driver and pit crew were introduced at the beach-road course at Daytona Beach, Florida, in 1952.**

speeds. NASCAR also runs the Craftsman Truck series for pickup trucks running at about 710 horsepower and speeds of up to 190 mph.

NASCAR racing focuses on wining racing series, not just individual races. The series winner is the driver with the most overall points at the end of the series. Points are awarded based on the driver's finish in each race. Each first-place win is worth 175 points. From first to sixth place, the points drop by five for each position—second place is worth 170 points, third is worth 165, and sixth is worth 150. From sixth down to twelfth, four points are deducted for each position—seventh place is worth 146 points and twelfth is worth 127. From thirteenth place down to forty-third place, three points are subtracted, with forty-third place being worth 34 points.

In addition to the points awarded for finishing position, five bonus points are awarded for leading a lap, plus five points for the driver who leads the most laps in a race.

As a result of this system, a driver may win more races than any other, but lose the racing series because another racer has collected more points.

THE FLAGS OF NASCAR

There are several different flags used by NASCAR officials to control each race. The best known is the checkered flag, indicating the end of the race and a win for the first driver to receive it. The next most common flags are the green and the yellow. Green indicates the beginning of or resumption of racing. It means the track is clear and the drivers should begin jockeying for position.

A yellow flag means a hazard exists on the track. If there's been an accident or if debris is present on the track, the flag is brought out. It may also be used when there is rain or bad weather, or if an emergency vehicle needs to cross the track. When the yellow flag is displayed, all vehicles are required to slow down and stay behind a pace car. On most tracks the yellow flag stays out for a minimum of three laps, allowing the cars to pit and regain their position before a restart.

The white flag indicates that there is one lap remaining in the race.

A red flag means that all competition, including the drivers and the pit crews, must stop, even if the crew is in the garage area repairing a car. This flag is most common during a significant rain delay or when the track is blocked by emergency vehicles or a particularly bad accident. A red flag will always be followed with a yellow flag to allow drivers to warm up their engines and pit if need be.

The black flag is the "consultation flag," and is given to a specific driver or drivers, not the entire group of racers. It means the driver must pull into the pit area to talk to race officials, usually because of a rule violation, or because the car is smoking, dropping pieces on the track, or not maintaining a minimum safe speed. If given the black flag, the driver must pit within five laps.

If a driver getting a black flag does not pit within five laps, he will get a black flag with a white X, which tells the driver he is disqualified.

The only optional flag in NASCAR is the blue flag with the orange diagonal stripe. If displayed, it tells a car or group of cars that the leaders are coming up behind them and they should move over to allow them to pass. Drivers may choose to ignore this flag, but NASCAR does not encourage this attitude.

High-Priced Sports

BASEBALL

Contrary to some popular myths, Abner Doubleday didn't "invent" baseball. It more or less evolved, tracing its base back to the English game of rounders. The sport was most often played by boys, and can be documented at least as far back as 1744.

Rounders is played on a pentagonal field with four posts. A batsman stood in a batting square twenty-eight feet from a "bowling square." A bowler threw a ball over the batting square, trying to place it above the knees and below the head of the batsman. The batsman was supposed to strike the ball and run around the posts. His goal was to make it all the way to the fourth post (which is located twenty-eight feet to the left of the batting square, and not colocated at the batting square as in baseball).

A runner was put out if a batted ball was caught, if he was tagged with the ball between posts, or the post to which he was running was tagged with the ball before he reached it. Players advanced

- **During the Second World War, between 1943 and 1945, the commissioner of baseball, Kennesaw Mountain Landis, established the "Potomac Line," which barred teams from training west of the Mississippi River or south of the Potomac River. The line was drawn up in conjunction with the U.S. Office of Defense Transportation to relieve loading on railways that were heavily engaged in transporting troops and war materiel.**
- **The original National League included teams in Chicago, Boston, Saint Louis, Hartford, Louisville, New York, Philadelphia, and Cincinnati.**
- **The Cincinnati Reds have changed stadiums more than any other pro baseball club.**
- **The Cincinnati Reds (then the Red Stockings) played in the first professional game of baseball (involving paid players) on June 1, 1869, against the Mansfield Independents. The Reds won 48 to 14.**

posts based on bad pitches (three to a batsman moved a runner to the next post) or hits. Reaching the fourth post was a rounder, worth one point. Rounders was played with nine players per team, with nine outs per inning and two innings per game.

This has enough in common with baseball that it is pretty hard to give any credence to the idea that Abner Doubleday "invented" the game. Rather, if he did originate it close to its current form in 1839 as he is alleged to have done, he was most likely working from the basis of rounders. There are some who claim that Doubleday was selected by a baseball committee with the sole goal of making it an "American" sport. Doubleday, a graduate of the U.S. Military Academy at West Point and a hero in the Civil War, fit the bill nicely.

Whatever the truth of the matter, the game was played in some form in the first half of the nineteenth century, and professional teams and leagues were established by the 1870s. The game as we know it really came into being in the middle of the twentieth century.

In 1947 Jackie Robinson started playing for the Brooklyn Dodgers, becoming the first African American to play in the major leagues, opening the door for other African Americans, Latinos, and Asians. This was the start of the game as a popular sport, crossing racial boundaries. The second major change was the move of the Dodgers and the Giants to the West Coast, expanding the game's reach beyond the East and Midwest.

Now that we've given lip service to the history of the game, go read the sidebar and let's get into something more interesting: uniform numbers.

UNIFORM NUMBERS

The 1916 Cleveland Indians were the first team to wear numbers. They wore them on the left sleeve, but ended the practice after a few weeks. The team tried again in 1917, with the numbers on the right sleeves this time. After a few weeks, they stopped. The St. Louis Cardinals tried numbers on the sleeves in 1923, and they too abandoned the idea.

Not surprisingly, uniform numbers were first worn permanently by the New York Yankees in 1929. The reason was to assist the fans in telling who was on the field. The initial numbers were assigned based on the player's batting number (Babe Ruth batted third, so he wore "3"). In 1932 the National League's (NL) president, John Heydler, issued instructions to all NL teams that they should take up the practice of uniform numbers. By 1935 almost all major league players wore numbers. The Philadelphia A's (an American League team) were the last team to take up the practice.

As an odd side note, all American League teams had taken to wearing numbers on the jerseys they wore on road games by 1931. The reason, one presumes, was so that fans unfamiliar with the visiting team could figure out who was who.

The most commonly retired numbers in Major League Baseball are, in descending order:

- 5—seven times so far
- 3, 4, and 14—six times so far
- 1 and 34—five times so far

The New York Yankees have retired the number 8 twice—once for Bill Dickey, once for Yogi Berra. The Expos did the same with the number 10, for Rusty Staub and Andre Dawson.

The New York Yankees have retired more numbers (fifteen) than any other major league team. The players or coaches and their numbers are:

Billy Martin   1

Babe Ruth   3

Lou Gehrig 4

Joe DiMaggio 5

Mickey Mantle 7

Bill Dickey 8

Yogi Berra 8

Roger Maris 9

Phil Rizzuto 10

Thurman Munson 15

Whitey Ford 16

Don Mattingly 23

Elston Howard 32

Casey Stengel 37

Reggie Jackson 44

EXPANSION HISTORY

From 1901 to 1960, the major leagues consisted of sixteen teams, evenly divided between the American and National Leagues. In 1961 the game started to expand:

1961: American League adds the Los Angeles Angels (later the California Angels and then the Anaheim Angels) and the Washington Senators (who replaced the original Senators, who moved to Minneapolis–St. Paul in 1960).

1962: National League adds New York Mets and Houston Colt .45s (later renamed the Astros).

1969: American League adds Kansas City Royals, Seattle Pilots. National League adds San Diego Padres, Montreal Expos. The Pilots last one season in Seattle before moving to Milwaukee to become the Brewers.

1972: Washington Senators move to Texas to become the Rangers.

1977: Toronto Blue Jays, Seattle Mariners added to the American League.

1993: National League adds Colorado Rockies, Florida Marlins.

1998: Major league team count reaches thirty with the Arizona Diamond-backs added to the NL and Tampa Bay Devil Rays to the AL.

FOOTBALL AMERICAN STYLE

American football traces its roots to the English game rugby, which started at the Rugby Boys' School in 1823, and to soccer, which is sometimes called association football, which also started in the 1820s in England. Like rugby, football uses an ovoid ball which must be advanced by running and passing into a goal area. In rugby, the ball must be touched down in the goal area. American football is not as fast moving as soccer and rugby, with stops and starts for each down.

Perhaps inspired by rugby and soccer, American college students began playing a game they called "ballown." Initially players used their fists to punch a ball forward, though they later added footwork. The sole goal of the game was to get the ball past the opposing team into a goal area. There were no real rules. The game was particularly popular at Harvard. The freshman and sophomore classes played the game on the first Monday of each school year. The day was known as "Bloody Monday," due to the extreme roughness of the game. Boston Common became the site of irregular games by 1860.

After the end of the Civil War, colleges began organizing regular football games, leading to the establishment of rules to keep the game from becoming total pandemonium. In 1869 Rutgers and Princeton played the first college game. Rutgers won six goals to four, using rules common at Rutgers (the home team). Princeton challenged for a rematch, played at Princeton with their rules, and beat Rutgers eight to nothing. In 1873 Columbia, Rutgers, Princeton, and Yale Universities sent representatives to New York to set out the formal rules for the game in intercollegiate play, and to establish the Intercollegiate Football Association (IFA). Around the same time team sizes were set at a maximum of fifteen players on each side, then reduced to eleven.

The IFA set many of the rules common to the game today, including the system of downs: at that time, it was three downs to go five yards. In 1906 this was changed to three downs to go ten yards. The fourth down was added in 1912, and the field was shortened to a hundred yards. The forward pass was introduced around the same time, resulting in a much more open style of play, which reduced injuries as well. Prior to this, the game had been more about brute force than finesse, and with almost no padding, the sport claimed many casualties through injury and several deaths—at least eighteen recorded.

The National Collegiate Athletic Association (NCAA) was founded in 1906, though the name was originally the Intercollegiate Athletic Association of the

• **The original American Professional Football Association (APFA) was founded in 1920, and included the following teams:**

- Akron Professionals
- Buffalo All-Americans
- Canton Bulldogs
- Chicago Cardinals
- Chicago Tigers (folded at the end of the 1920 season)
- Cleveland Tigers (folded after the 1921 season)
- Columbus Panhandles
- Dayton Triangles
- Decatur Staleys
- Detroit Heralds (folded after the 1921 season)
- Hammond Pros
- Muncie Flyers (folded after the 1921 season)
- Rochester (New York) Jeffersons
- Rock Island Independents

• **In 1943 the Philadelphia Eagles and the Pittsburgh Steelers merged (for the 1943 season only). In 1945 the Brooklyn Tigers and the Boston Yanks merged for one season.**

United States (IAAUS). The title was changed in 1910. The NCAA was also responsible for setting the current game length (sixty minutes), and for setting the neutral zone separation between the teams.

Professional football can trace its roots to college. The American Professional Football Association (AFPA) was formed in 1920 (professional games had been played as early as 1895, though the structure was informal) with twenty-three teams. In 1922 the APFA changed its name to the National Football League (NFL). The American Football League (AFL) was formed in 1960, and the two merged into one in 1970, combining sixteen NFL and ten AFL teams.

Professional football had other fits and starts other than the NFL, such as the All-American Football Conference and the World Football League, and Arena Football—which is still played but is not exactly what you'd call popular.

THE DIFFERENCE BETWEEN THE NFL AND THE CFL

The most essential difference between the NFL and the CFL is, of course, that one is American and the other Canadian, though that doesn't extend to the players. Warren Moon, the Rose Bowl–winning quarterback from the University of Washington back in the 1970s and former Houston Oiler great, played in the CFL, winning six Gray Cups (or *Coupe Gris*, if you insist on that bilingual stuff they do up there). Doug Flutie is also a CFL alumnus. The CFL picks draft choices from U.S. universities in its own draft, and players migrate back and forth, some on the way up, others moving into the twilight of their careers. It even made an attempt at an extension of the CFL in the United States in 1994, but this died as quickly as it started (it was all over by 1995).

CFL-style football uses twelve players per side on a field that is the same general layout and markings as an American-style gridiron, but 10 yards longer and 11.5 yards wider. Instead of four downs to get a first down, only three are allowed in the CFL. This encourages a wide-open offense with lots of passing, but also means that there tends to be more punting than in American-style games.

Scoring is essentially the same in both leagues, with one twist. In the CFL, teams may score "singles," for a single point. They are also called the "rouge." Singles are awarded when the ball enters a goal area after a punt or missed field goal and is downed by a defensive player, or the ball goes out of bounds from the goal area. Singles are also scored on kickoff if the ball is touched by a member of the opposing team and then enters the goal area.

There are a few other basic differences. The NFL allows for six time-outs (three per half), whereas the CFL only allows one per half. Also, the NFL plays fifteen-minute sudden-death overtime periods—first team to score in the overtime wins. The CFL plays two ten-minute overtime periods, with the winner being the team with the highest score at the end of the two periods. In the event of the teams still being tied, another pair of ten-minute periods are played, and so on until a winner emerges.

NFL END ZONE DANCES—ORIGIN AND RULES

The issue of post-scoring celebration in football, specifically after touchdowns, has been a long and unpleasant debate in football.

End-zone celebrations got a late start in the NFL. In 1966 a New York Giants wide receiver, Homer Jones, spiked the ball after scoring a touchdown. That is the first recorded case of the spike, which is the most basic form of end-zone celebration, and it caught on in the league.

Eight years later, on November 18, 1973, Elmo Wright of the Kansas City Chiefs caught a pass for a touchdown from quarterback Len Dawson in a 38–14 win over the Houston Oilers. After the referee signaled the touchdown, Wright ran in place for a few moments, then slammed the ball into the ground. Simple, primitive, to the point—and the start of real celebration.

It was up to a rookie, Billy "White Shoes" Johnson, of the Houston Oilers, to transform Wright's simple celebration into something more, something that would become both a permanent part of the game and a point of contention. Johnson, after a touchdown pass, performed his own version of the funky chicken, including rolling the ball along his arms, bringing dance to the NFL. His performances inspired others to try their own hand at displays of celebration, beginning a secondary form of competition in the end zone.

Then came back flips and goal-post dunking (leaping and flipping the ball over the crossbar of the goal post), dances, and more. In some cases, it was clear from the large groups involved and the complexity of the routines that they were rehearsed and choreographed ahead of time—which suggested to the league that it wasn't so much a spontaneous celebration of joy as a bit of showboating.

The dances even crept out of the end zone. Many players, when a touchdown was assured, would switch from straight-ahead running to a high-stepping glide, frequently pointing backward at and taunting the pursuing defense with the ball.

In 1984 the NFL responded to this with rules regarding "excessive celebration," limiting the show to little more than a spike in the end zone (many players then started celebrating afterward on their own sideline), prompting many to claim that "NFL" stood for "No Fun League." Regardless, excessive celebration was cause for a fifteen-yard penalty against the offending team.

In 1991 the rule was amended to prohibit celebrations that involved taunting, specifically "the use of baiting or taunting acts or words that engender ill will between teams." This loosened up things enough that celebrations, within reason and good taste, were allowed.

Some of the better-known celebrations include the Bronco's mile-high salute, the Atlanta Falcons' dirty bird, the Green Bay Packers' Lambeau leap, and the Ickey shuffle, performed by Cincinnati's Ickey Woods.

HOCKEY

Hockey shares a lot in common with soccer and lacrosse, in that it is a game of moving the puck up the field of play and trying to get past the defense to score. Like soccer and lacrosse, there is a goalie protecting the goal, and like lacrosse, the players get to assault the puck (and one another) with sticks.

Hockey can be traced to northern Europe, its roots being based in a variety of warm-weather games similar to field hockey. During winter months, players used frozen fields, marshland, or ponds to continue playing. There are historical references from the seventeenth century to a hockey-like ice game called kolven, played in Holland. An English version of the game, known as bandy, was reported in English newspapers in 1820.

As the English settled Canada, they brought the sport with them. British soldiers played the game in Halifax, Nova Scotia, and students at McGill University in Montreal are reported to have been playing informal

- Most experts agree that the common name for the sport comes from the French word *hoquet*, meaning a shepherd's crook, based on the similarity in shape between the crook and the hockey stick.

- Hockey pucks are made of vulcanized rubber, measure three inches in diameter, and weigh six ounces. They are frozen before being used in a game to prevent bouncing.

- Names of individuals and teams are inscribed on the Stanley Cup. Misspellings have occurred and with one exception have not been corrected. For example, in 1972 the name of the Boston Bruins was spelled "Bqstqn Bruins."

- A really hard full-body hockey check, by a couple of two-hundred-pounders colliding at a combined speed of twenty miles per hour, produces enough energy to light up a 60-watt bulb for thirty seconds.

games in the 1870s. There is also new evidence indicating that the sport may have started in Windsor, Nova Scotia, at a place called Long Pond. The pond is still there, and is almost exactly the dimensions of a National Hockey League (NHL) rink.

Given the mix of opinions as to the site of the "first game," and claims that the sport takes its roots from the Native American game lacrosse, it is impossible to exactly determine when hockey as we know it began. Nevertheless, it appears that the sport took hold, particularly in North America, before the end of the nineteenth century.

The first Canadian hockey league was formed in Kingston with four clubs, which played nine men a side (though this varied from place to place and league to league). By 1893 teams played with seven men a side. As of 2003, the National Hockey League consists of thirty teams divided equally into two conferences (Eastern and Western).

THE STANLEY CUP

The Stanley Cup was named after Baron Stanley of Preston, governor general of Canada, and was awarded commencing in 1893 to the annual amateur hockey champion of Canada. As such, the Stanley Cup is the oldest trophy in professional sports competition in North America. After 1917 the cup was awarded to the champion of the National Hockey League (the Toronto Arenas beat the Vancouver Millionaires three games to two in the best-of-five series that year).

The following year there was no winner as the series was called off between the Montreal Canadiens and the Seattle Metropolitans (due to the influenza epidemic that was killing many thousands).

As of this writing, the Montreal Canadiens have won the Stanley Cup more times than any other team, a total of twenty-four times.

ICE

Hockey rinks generally make ice by pumping freezing brine (salt water) through pipes in a concrete slab. As the slab gets cold, water is poured onto it, forming layers of ice. The markings for the game are painted on lower layers. More layers are frozen above them, to make a surface about three-quarters to one inch thick.

Perfect ice for hockey should be maintained at 16°F. For figure skating, 22°F is preferred. Apparently figure skaters prefer softer ice for their landings. Or maybe they're just wimps. Fast ice is colder and smoother, whereas slow ice is warmer and mushier.

BASKETBALL

The Boston Celtics are not the greatest basketball team ever. Sorry, but the facts just don't support that. The first all-black professional basketball team, the New York Renaissance (known as the "Rens"), deserve that title.

The Rens were formed in 1923 by Bob Douglas (called the "father of black basketball" by the Naismith Memorial Basketball Hall of Fame), taking their name from the Harlem Renaissance Casino, which had opened the year before. In exchange for the free publicity the casino received, the Rens got a place to practice and play home games.

The American Basketball League refused the Rens admittance in 1925. (Their greatest rivals, the original Celtics, then refused to join the ABL in a show of support.) In spite of this, the Rens played against a wide variety of teams, including pro, semipro, and black college teams. They defeated the Celtics twice for the World Basketball championship (during the 1932–33 season, when the ABL had suspended operations due to the Great Depression). During the 1932 season, the Rens won 112 out of 120 games, including a winning streak of 88 games (the Celtics' record streak stands at 44 games).

The Rens were purchased in 1949 by Abe Saperstein, the founder and owner of the team that would become the Harlem Globetrotters (see sidebar "Saperstein's New York Globetrotters"). The Rens defeated the Globetrotters in 1939 in the World Basketball Championships.

The Rens played from 1923 until 1949, compiling a record of 2,588 wins against 529 losses.

- The International Basketball Federation (the international governing body for basketball) has 212 member countries. This is more than there are members of the UN (currently only 191 nations) or UN members that signed the Nuclear Nonproliferation Treaty (188).
- Basketball became an Olympic sport at the 1936 Olympic Games held in Berlin in 1936.

SAPERSTEIN'S NEW YORK GLOBETROTTERS

In 1926 Abe Saperstein organized a basketball team named the Savoy Big Five (named after the Chicago Savoy Ballroom). The ballroom, which was hurting for business, started hosting basketball games and agreed to sponsor Saperstein's team. The team was not an attraction and was disbanded; however, several members rejoined Saperstein's new team the following year.

On January 7, 1927, the team played its first game in Hinckley, Illinois. They wore uniforms with the words NEW YORK on them. Shortly thereafter, Saperstein renamed them "Saperstein's New York Globetrotters." It wasn't until 1930 that the team was named the Harlem Globetrotters, in recognition of the fact that all the players were black. (In fact, the Globetrotters didn't play their first game in Harlem until 1968.)

Technically speaking, Saperstein was the first white to play with the Globetrotters, as he suited up and played in some games when other players were hurt or tired. Bob Karstens became the first white player under contract in 1942, replacing Goose Tatum, who joined the Army Air Corps. Karstens came from Dubuque, Iowa, and was known as a superb ball handler. Karstens helped develop some of the Globetrotters' signature gags and routines, including the "magic circle" pregame warm-up, the "goofball" (a ball filled with off-center weights), and the "yo-yo" basketball.

TWENTY-FOUR-SECOND RULE

Prior to the 1954–55 season, there was no twenty-four-second shot clock. Teams could hang on to the ball as long as they wanted to, forcing the other team to foul. The result was low-score games and an excess of free throws: in 1950, in a game between the Pistons and Lakers, the score was 19–18, with a total of eight baskets scored between the two teams. In one playoff game in 1953, 106 fouls were called and 128 free throws were shot.

Danny Biasone, owner of the Syracuse Nationals, introduced the idea of the shot clock, giving a team twenty-four seconds to attempt a shot or else lose possession of the ball. To deal with excessive fouling, the NBA board of governors adopted rules limiting the number of fouls per team per quarter, with each foul becoming a shooting foul after the limit was reached. At five fouls, a player was out of the game.

- **Dr. Henry Kissenger, former secretary of state, was named the Globetrotters' first honorary team member in 1976.**
- **Wilt Chamberlain started his pro career as a Globetrotter in 1958, before joining the NBA in 1959.**
- **The first official three-point shot in college basketball history was made on November 29, 1980, by Ronnie Carr from West Carolina. West Carolina went on to win the game (against Middle Tennessee State) 77–70.**
- **During some professional basketball games early in the twentieth century, there was no "out-of-bounds," as the entire court was surrounded by wire meshing.**

Not So Professional Sports

RODEO

The sport of competitive rodeo evolved from the working lifestyle of the western American cowboy. Competitions were organized between rival ranches when cowboys were gathered in one place, usually before or after cattle drives. Many rodeo events come from everyday work requirements such as roping, while others may have their roots in one cowboy daring another to try something difficult or stupid. Bull riding, for example, has very little practical application in day-to-day ranch activities.

The birthplace of the rodeo is a controversial subject among those who follow the sport. Prescott, Arizona, and Pecos, Texas, both claimed to be, though the matter did not come to a head until the makers of the game Trivial Pursuit included a question about where the rodeo started (Prescott, according to the game maker). Pecos's rodeo supporters and historians objected, but they agreed with their counterparts in Prescott to allow the game maker to research the matter more thoroughly and abide by the results.

The game maker determined that Prescott was in fact the site of the first *formal* rodeo, retaining this as the correct answer in the game; however, the city of Pecos website continues to quote the 1961 edition of the *Encyclopaedia Britannica*, which supported their initial claim. The entry in that volume read, "The first public contest for prizes for bronco riding and steer roping was held in Pecos, Texas, on July 4, 1883. No admission was charged."

Regardless of the definition of a true rodeo and the birthplace, rodeos remain popular across the west and even east of the Mississippi—there is a rodeo in Arcadia, Florida (which claims to be the "grand daddy of 'em all," even though it started in 1929).

RODEO EVENTS

The rodeo typically consists of eight events:

Saddle Bronc Racing: A cowboy rides a horse with saddle and is judged on style and a mandatory eight-second ride. The cowboy must rake his spurs across the horse's flanks toward the cantle of the saddle (the cantle is the slightly raised rear edge of the saddle). The judges look for the rider's feet to sweep forward even with the horse's shoulders at the same time the horse's front feet strike the ground. Points are awarded to a maximum of twenty-five.

Bareback Riding: An invented rodeo sport. The rider must stay on the horse for eight seconds, keeping one hand in the air above his head. Touching the horse with his free hand or allowing the hand to make contact with any part of the cowboy results in a disqualification. The cowboy's spurs must make contact with the horse's shoulders when the horse's front feet touch the ground, with the feet swinging back to the rigging harness that is used by the cowboy to hold on to the horse. Points are awarded up to a maximum of twenty-five.

Team Roping: A pair of cowboys, a "header" and a "heeler," each mount a horse. The header chases the steer and lassos it around the horns, turning it so the heeler can lasso the steer's hind legs. The ropes are secured to the saddle horns, and the two horses turn to face each other with the ropes tight and the steer between them, at which point time is called.

Calf Roping: A roping event. One cowboy chases down a calf and ropes it. As soon as the rope is thrown and around the calf's neck, the cowboy jerks the rope to close the loop. He jumps from his horse, pushes the calf over, tying any three legs up. Fastest time wins.

Steer Wrestling: A cowboy and an assistant, called a "hazer" chase a steer. The hazer keeps the steer running straight, but may not touch the steer. The cowboy catches the steer, brings it to a complete stop, and wrestles it to the ground with all four legs pointing in the same direction. The steers are required to weigh between 450 and 750 pounds, and the event is won by the best time.

Barrel Racing: A cowgirl sport. Three barrels are set up twenty to thirty yards apart in a triangular pattern, and the cowgirls race on their horses around them in a cloverleaf pattern. Fastest time wins.

Bull Riding: A rider must stay on the bull for the full eight seconds, holding on with one hand to a rope strung around the bull just behind the shoulders. Some bull riding is done without a rope, making the ride exceedingly difficult. The rider's other hand must be kept in the air above his head and may not touch the bull or the rider. The rider is awarded points up to a maximum of twenty-five, based on style and form, relative to the difficulty of the bull drawn.

Bullfighting: An extension of rodeo clowning, bullfighting was started in 1980. Professional rodeo clowns fight bulls for at least forty seconds, with an additional thirty seconds optional. The bulls are smaller and faster than the bulls used in bull riding and have the capacity to learn the moves of the clowns, improving with experience. Judges award points based on the skill of the fighter and the aggressiveness of the bull.

THE NENANA ICE CLASSIC

In the winter of 1917, a group of engineers building a bridge across the Tanana River for the Alaska Railroad were idled by ice and snow. With little else to do, the engineers started a betting pool on the time the ice would take to break up enough for construction to restart. This marked the first Nenana Ice Classic. In contemporary times, the Ice Classic has become a formalized event, drawing many thousands of entries from both in and out of Alaska.

A black-and-white striped log tripod is frozen in place on the ice in the river approximately three hundred feet from shore near the rail bridge. A watchtower is set up to monitor the tripod. A wire extending from the tripod is connected to a continuously running clock. When the tripod reaches a point one hundred feet from its original location due to ice movement, the wire triggers the clock to stop. This has been set as the definition of breakup. A siren is set off when the first movement occurs to notify the townspeople.

Betting is open to anyone interested. Bets can be placed by writing to the Nenana Ice Classic in Nenana, Alaska, with a guess as to the specific date and time (Alaska time, including hour and minute) you believe the breakup will happen—remember to indicate a.m. or p.m. for the time. Bets are $2 each, and the number of bets is unlimited. The deadline for the bets is in early April.

The most common winning date is April 30, followed by April 29. The historical data show the best time of day has been between 1:00 p.m. and 1:59 p.m., and 3:00 p.m. and 3:59 p.m. Climatologists recommend factoring in current weather trends and global warming when selecting a date and time to bet on.

The original betting pool was $800 in 1917. The 2001 pool was worth $308,000 and was split eight ways.

SWAMP BUGGY RACING

Swamp buggy racing traces its roots back to the 1930s, to the boggy areas common in the coastal areas of the southeastern United States. These areas aren't solid enough to be suitable for wheeled vehicles, and aren't wet enough for boats. A hybrid vehicle, the swamp buggy, using balloon tires fitted to a boatlike body, emerged as the most suitable means of crossing swamps. Over time, they became a regular means of transportation.

Racing the buggies started when hunters gathered in the swamps before the start of hunting season. The sportsmen spent time tinkering with their machines, tuning, testing, and prepping them. Racing was inevitable. The first official race was held in 1949 in Naples, Florida, which has since become the sport's home. Community leaders organized "Swamp Buggy Days," including a parade and other festivities.

Swamp buggy racetracks are more or less oval in shape and are covered with one to five feet of water, including a deep spot known as the "sippy hole."

Swamp buggies are equipped with large, narrow front wheels with a set of skis behind them to help the buggy lift up out of the water and decrease drag. Rear wheels are heavier and thicker, equipped with heavy treads to bite into the muck on the bottom of the course. (Jeeps are also raced.)

Swamp buggy races include the crowning of the swamp buggy queen, whose primary function (aside from presiding over all racing activities) is the swamp buggy queen's annual mudbath. The queen is picked up like a new bride by the racing winner and dumped into the sippy hold. This tradition started in 1957 when that year's winner, H. W. McCurry, grabbed the queen (who was still wearing her gown), and dunked her in the muckiest part of the famous "Mile O' Mud" oval racetrack.

SWAMP BUGGY RACING RULES

If you're gonna race a swamp buggy, you can be disqualified for:

- Crowding—driving a buggy such that it intentionally denies another buggy room to make a legitimate attempt at passing.

- Blocking—similar to crowding, involving moving in front of another buggy without allowing adequate room for the trailing driver to take evasive action.
- Running the banks—a buggy driving with two or more wheels up on the exposed ground outside the track, the track being defined as those portions of the racecourse covered with water. If the buggy in question is forced out by another buggy but returns to the track immediately without gaining unfair advantage, the judges will take no action.

TRACTOR PULLS

The first image that may come to mind at the words "tractor pull" might be a tug-of-war between two tractors. Tractor pulls *are* about brute strength, but in a different way.

A tractor, which may be a truck, a customized vehicle, or a stock tractor, is hitched to a device called a sled. The sled is loaded with a set amount of weight that is initially placed at the back of the sled over its rear wheels. Once a start signal is given the tractor races forward, and the weight begins to shift forward, transferring more and more pressure to a skid plate at the front end of the sled. Unless the tractor is particularly powerful and the weight low enough, the increasing pressure on the skid plate causes friction to increase until it overcomes the ability of the tractor to move forward.

Typically, two tractors race simultaneously on a dirt track, but they're going for distance, not speed. (Failure to go at least 100 feet is grounds for disqualification.) Indoor tracks are between 150 and 300 feet, but outdoor tracks are always 300 feet long. The winner of any given contest is the machine that goes the farthest up to the length of the track.

How and where pulling started depends on which of the several tractor-pull associations you consult with. There are at least two competing groups in the United States, the National Tractor Pullers Association (NTPA) and the American Tractor Pullers Association (ATPA), plus several overseas (including Europe and Australia). Anyplace you might find heavy-duty agricultural machines combined with gearheads seems to spawn tractor pulls. Regardless, all parties agree that the sport is American in origin and started in the late 1920s.

PENTACOST ISLAND LAND DIVING

Land diving is done on Pentacost primarily to bless the soil. The Pentacost Islanders build towers up to eighty feet tall and leap from the top with vines tied to their ankles as part of spiritual and religious celebrations. Properly performed, this act of faith and manhood breaks the jumper's fall just before he would hit the ground, sparing him injury or death.

If a diver can skim the earth with the top of his head, he is assured fertile soil and a good harvest (predominantly yams). This is also a test of manhood, required of boys when they have reached puberty. In this case, the boy's mother watches from the ground holding a favorite toy or item from the boy's childhood. After the boy completes his jump, the item is discarded, symbolizing the end of childhood.

Men often use the time before dives to settle disputes or repair relationships, in the event they are killed. It is traditional to abstain from sex for at least a day before the leap, and lucky charms are not worn.

THE DANGEROUS SPORTS CLUB

Bungee jumping as a sport began with a group of Oxford students in the late 1970s. This group was inspired by the land diving performed by the people of Pentecost Island in the South Pacific. (No one knows exactly why a bunch of Oxford students were checking out Pentecost Island—perhaps they were checking through back issues of *National Geographic* in search of pictures of naked Polynesian women and came across land diving.)

The Oxford students chose to use elastic bungee cords in place of vines. Rather than build a tower, the group (which has formalized itself into the Dangerous Sports Club, or DSC) made the first bungee jump from the Clifton Suspension Bridge in England on April 1, 1977. The participants were arrested. Until the 1990s, the sport was banned in the United Kingdom due to legalities, but became a hit elsewhere.

The DSC has continued to undertake both exceptionally dangerous and unique challenges, including dining on the top of a hot air balloon and crossing the English Channel in a septic tank. One of their most recent undertakings was building and using the "human trebuchet." The trebuchet is a type of siege weapon used many hundreds of years ago to throw rocks and other items at or into forts and walled cities. In the case of the DSC's version, it throws people into a net. Only one serious injury has been reported to date, when a rider bounced out of the net into a mud puddle (which reportedly broke her fall, but caused the aid car sent to retrieve her to get stuck for a time).

JUMPING TIDBITS

Bungee jumping requires a harness (either a full-body harness or a leg harness), a bungee (essentially a large rubber band), and something to leap off of.

Ways to Bungee

Straight Jump: Leaping off a high object and rebounding. This is the original and most common.

Catapult: This is essentially inverted bungee jumping, being fired up by the tension on the cords rather than dropping. This is typically done with two parallel towers or objects with a gap in the middle to prevent the jumper from striking something hard on the upward path.

Dives

Back Dive: Face away from the jump and fall backward with the head leading. This is a difficult dive for beginners.

Bat Dive: The diver is held facedown by the feet from the tower or jump point, then released.

Swallow Dive: A swallow dive is accomplished by facing forward and leaping out, arms outstretched. This is the most common way to dive.

Pile Driver: Similar to the Bat, except you drop feet-first straight down. Divers may also jump in tandem or be thrown.

THE DEMOLITION DERBY

The history of the demolition derby, like that of so many sports, is not exact. None of the several competing organizations that claim to represent the sport agree on the where or when it started, but anecdotal evidence suggests that it started in the 1930s. One story says it was the inspiration of a man who witnessed a particularly belligerent exchange of pushing, shoving, and ramming by cars and drivers following a car accident in Chicago. The passerby noted that pedestrians were riveted, watching the exchange, and he figured he could get people to pay to see the same sort of thing on a larger, controlled scale.

The specific rules of a demolition derby vary from place to place, taking into account insurance and liability requirements, local ordinances and codes, and the sensitivities of the promoters.

Generally, the guidelines for a demo-derby are:

- A demo-derby takes place on a track, often little more than a dirt field enclosed by barriers to prevent the cars from escaping into the spectator area and causing injury.
- Drivers compete in qualifying heats or feature races, with the basic goal of crashing into or hitting other cars and disabling them without becoming disabled themselves.
- The winner is the driver of the last car able to move after colliding with a car that is unable to move under its own power.
- The rules also require that cars must aim to collide with alternating opponents to prevent multiple drivers from ganging up on individuals or teams of drivers.

Safety precautions in the sport are extensive. Drivers are, for example, prohibited from striking another vehicle on the driver's door. Fires in the engine compartment or driver's compartment disqualify a vehicle, and safety equipment such as seat belts, crash helmets, fireproof suits, protection for the fuel tank and battery, and reinforcement of the driver's door are all standard. While injuries do happen, one expert source reports that they are more apt to occur in the pit areas than on the track, largely because of the fast pace of the work done there and the close quarters the pit crews and cars occupy.

BUILDING A DEMO-DERBY CAR—TIPS FROM A PRO

Building a winning demo-derby car is not as simple as running a junker on the track. Experienced drivers practice a lot of common sense and good engineering when preparing a car for the event. A few key tips:

- Strip the car completely. Any material that is unnecessary should be taken out. Any material that can catch fire must be removed.
- Cut extra clearance in the body around the tires.
- Remove the hood latching mechanism and use wire, chains, or bolts to close the hood. The hood latch mechanism will not work after it has been hit a few times.
- The alternator can be removed if the battery is fully charged and good quality. Removing the alternator will prevent the battery from grounding out.
- Use a good battery and protect it in a wooden box. Metal boxes gouge the casing.
- Cover all wires and cables with split lengths of garden hose to protect them.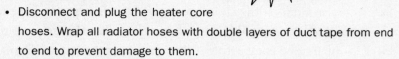
- Metal boat fuel tanks are the best in place of the original gas tank.
- Disconnect and plug the heater core hoses. Wrap all radiator hoses with double layers of duct tape from end to end to prevent damage to them.
- Add stop-lead to the radiator fluid.
- Reinforce your motor mount to prevent it from snapping.
- Install a transmission fluid cooler if allowed. Either route cooling from the radiator or run the fluid in tubes through a box packed with dry ice.
- Run the tallest and narrowest tires possible.
- Put a washer behind one lug nut on the drive tires. This gives the wheel a slight wobble and improves traction.

- Vacuum the interior thoroughly before competing to keep loose debris from being stirred up and interfering with visibility.
- Do not arrive early at the track. Judges will inspect all cars, and the later arrivals get the least attention.
- Over fifty thousand people compete in the United States at county fairs, racetracks, and other events.
- The school bus demolition derby is an offshoot of the traditional demolition derby, with similar rules. School buses "back" off in an arena. Unlike traditional derbies, the buses smack into each other back end first, sometimes hard enough to crush a bus all the way to its rear axle.

LAWN MOWER RACING

Lawn mower racing seems like the thing that a group of midwestern gearheads might come up with on a lazy Sunday afternoon. Nothing could be further from the truth.

The British Lawn Mower Association (BLMA) was founded in the Cricketers Arms, Wisborough Green, in 1973. According to the BLMA's official history:

> Back when the world was young and at least beer was still cheap these chaps were sitting in the Cricketers Arms. "We need a cheap motor sport," said one. "Everybody has a lawn mower," said Jim Gavin [a future lawn racing legend], "let's race those." So they did, and it was good!

The BLMA allows racing in three separate classes (rather than two as in the United States): the unpowered walk-behind, the powered walk-behind, and the driving mower (called a riding mower in the United States).

The United States Lawn Mower Racing Association (USLMRA)

was founded when executives from the American maker of a fuel additive witnessed the activities of the British Lawn Mower Association in 1992 in England and thought it might be a fun activity to introduce to the United States. Nowadays, the USLMRA runs more than twenty racing events across the country, including races on closed one-eighth-mile tracks (usually 20 laps or 2.5 miles) and drag races on a 150-foot straightaway. And while some might initially scoff at the idea of racing mere lawn mowers, most of the doubters have not seen the racing mowers running at 30 to 60 mph.

• The BLMA and the USLMRA met in 2000 to compete. The BLMA won.

Typical requirements for racing are straightforward and put safety first. USLMRA rules:

- You need to be a member in good standing of the USLMRA.
- You must be at least eighteen years of age, or have parental permission if you are sixteen or seventeen.
- You have to sign a liability release.
- Racing is open to all self-propelled rotary or reel-style riding lawn mowers that are still suitable for cutting grass, within the modifications allowed by the USLMRA handbook. The mower must have been originally designed and sold commercially to mow lawns.
- Racing mowers in an USLMRA event must be inspected and approved, and may be reinspected by the chief steward or chief technical inspector.
- Cutting blades must be removed from all mowers.
- Nonstock mowers must be equipped with an automatic throttle closing device or kill switch.
- All mowers must be equipped with an engine safety cutoff switch.

- At least two wheels must have brakes, and they must be in good condition.
- Engine fuel must be pump gas (the type sold at a commercial fueling station). The only additive allowed is STA-BIL Fuel Stabilizer (made by the company that started the sport in the United States, and which remains one of the primary sponsors).
- Every driver must wear an automobile racing or motorcycle-type safety helmet.
- Long-sleeved shirt, long pants, gloves, and shoes are required when on the track.

The USLMRA recognizes four basic classes of racing mower. These are:

- Stock, as delivered from the factory.
- IMOW (International Mower of Weeds), with a front engine, highly regulated.
- Prepared class, which allows for modified drive train, engine, etc. Subcategories are referred to as B, S, and A class, depending on motors and sizes.
- FX class, which allows for major modifications.

Games

POKER

Poker is a card game, believed to have originated in Asia. There are 2,598,960 possible poker hands with a fifty-two-card deck. Under most commonly accepted rules, poker hands are ranked, in descending order, as follows:

FIVE OF A KIND: Wild cards required.

ROYAL FLUSH: Ace-king-queen-jack-ten, all in the same suit.

STRAIGHT FLUSH: Five cards in numeric sequence and in the same suit.

FOUR OF A KIND

FULL HOUSE: A combination of five cards, two with one face value (two sevens, for example), and three with another face value (three jacks, for example). Also called a "barn" or "full boat."

FLUSH: Five cards of the same suit but not in sequence.

STRAIGHT: Five cards in sequence, such as seven-eight-nine-ten-jack.

THREE OF A KIND

TWO PAIR

ONE PAIR

SUCKING WIND (nothing): If no better hands are showing, the hand with the highest card takes the pot.

There are a few special hands—these are not well known and played rarely (they're kind of girl hands, like using wild cards). These are:

SKIP STRAIGHT: Alternating cards in sequence, such as queen-ten-eight-six-four, or king-jack-nine-seven-five. This beats three of a kind, but loses to a traditional straight.

ROUND THE CORNER STRAIGHT: A straight that wraps from the lower cards to the higher cards. For example, four-three-two-ace-king or three-two-ace-king-queen. The higher the low card, the better the hand (so four-three-two-ace-king beats three-two-ace-king-queen), and the skip straight ranks above the round the corner.

BOBTAIL STRAIGHT: A straight of four cards, with an "open end" that can be filled either high or low with another card. For example, seven-six-five-four is a bobtail because an eight or a three will complete it. Four-three-two-ace is not because only a five will complete it. A bobtail beats one pair but loses to two pair.

Standard draw poker involves each player being dealt one card per player, moving clockwise from the dealer with the dealer getting the last card, until each player has received five cards. Cards are dealt facedown. After the first round of betting, some versions of the game allow a player to discard and draw new cards, usually no more than four.

In stud poker each player gets a combination of cards facedown

- The world's largest manufacturer of playing cards is the United States Playing Card Company (USPC), based in Norwood, Ohio. The Bicycle brand has been in continuous production since 1885.

- During the Second World War, the USPC manufactured cards to be sent to American prisoners of war in relief packages. The cards, when moistened, could be peeled apart to reveal maps of escape routes to be used by the prisoners.

- During the Vietnam War, American soldiers were supplied with special decks of cards containing only the ace of spades. The Viet Cong were said to be very frightened of this card (during the French occupation of Indochina, the Vietnamese had learned that the ace of spades meant death in French fortune telling) and U.S. forces dropped them in enemy held areas to demoralize the enemy.

- The joker first appeared in cards in about 1865 and originated in America.

- James Butler "Wild Bill" Hickok was shot in the back of the head by James McCall during a poker game at Carl McCann's saloon in Deadwood, Dakota Territory. Hickok was holding two aces and two eights (the suit of these cards and the suit and value of the fifth card have never been conclusively established), which has since become known as the "dead man's hand."

and faceup. Similar to draw poker, cards are dealt clockwise one per player, with the first card (called the hole card) almost always being dealt facedown. The most common forms of stud poker require seven cards, with the first two down, four faceup, and the final card facedown. Discards are generally not allowed. Given the higher card count, stud poker lends itself to more variations such as high-low (a game in which a player may bet that he has the highest or the lowest five-card hand, or sometimes both).

SLOT MACHINES

Charles Fey is often credited with inventing the slot machine in 1896. Variations of the machine predate this, but Fey was apparently the first to develop it as a gambling device, rather than the simple amusement machine it was originally intended to be.

A slot machine is a box with a machine containing three or more reels. The surfaces of the reels are covered with a variety of symbols.

The player feeds a coin or token into the machine and pulls a lever arm to set the reels spinning (modern machines use push buttons). The reels spin, slowing according to the actions of governors, and stop. Payout to the player is determined by what combination of symbols align under a marked line on the front cover of the machine. Some early machines were designed to provide a payout when a certain weight of coins had been deposited, but smart players soon realized this mechanical trigger could be actuated by jostling the machines.

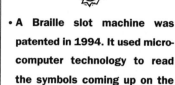

- A Braille slot machine was patented in 1994. It used microcomputer technology to read the symbols coming up on the machine's dials and translate them into raised Braille images.

Some versions of slot machines were put in grocery stores and other shops, dispensing tokens that could be traded for goods at the stores. This version was known as a "trade simulator."

GOLF

At first glance, golf doesn't seem like a guy sport. More of the Ken-and-Spalding, country club, plaid pants scene. (Think the tightass crowd in *Caddy Shack* and you've got the image.) On the other hand, golf was invented by a bunch of rough-and-tumble badasses from Scotland, the same ones who brought us single-malt whiskey and Mel Gibson looking tough as hell—in a skirt. You can play golf on a mountain in Alaska or on an ice floe in Greenland.

Face it, guys and golf go together like blondes and southern California beaches!

GOLF—THE GENERAL RUNDOWN

The Scots claim to be the fathers of golf, and evidence for the game starting in Scotland is strong; however, there are historic records of other games similar to golf: the Romans played something like golf, smacking a feather-stuffed ball around with a stick, and the Dutch played something similar as far back as the fifteenth century (on frozen canals). Regardless of this, arguing with a Scotsman about anything is both a waste of time and dangerous, so I hereby declare the Scots to be the fathers of golf.

The game caught on with the greatest enthusiasm among the Scottish, so much so that in 1457 Parliament banned it because it interfered with archery practice (a necessity for national defense in those days). Naturally the Scots ignored the ban, and golf continued as a very popular illegal activity until 1502, when King James IV solved the problem between government and golfer by joining the ranks of those addicted to the sport.

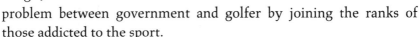

The oldest golf course in the world is Saint Andrew's, located in Scotland. Not that Saint Andrew's was always treated with the almost holy degree of respect it has today. In 1799 it was sold to a rabbit farmer as a place to breed and raise his stock. In 1821 local landowner James Cheape bought the land back. Saint Andrew's also claims the distinction of creating the 18-hole course standard that is still used today. In 1764 the "old course" was 22 holes, 11 out and 11 back. In truth, it was only 12, but holes 1 to 10 were the same as 12 to 21. Players complained that four of the holes were too short, so they were used to make fewer, longer holes, thus bringing the number to 18.

• Golf was played at the 1900 Olympics. The gold medals were taken by Charles Sands and Margaret Abbot, both Americans. Golf was also included in the 1904 Olympics, but was dropped after that. Probably due to a protest by the Scots . . .

GOLF BALL HISTORY AND AERODYNAMICS

The original ball was a leather sack filled with goose feathers. The leather was moistened, and then stuffed with the feathers (which were also wet). When the ball was as full as it could get, it was sewn shut and allowed to dry and harden and then oiled. A well-made ball of this type could be driven up to about 170 yards. Unfortunately, the ball, called a feathery, was useless when wet, which was pretty much all the time in Scotland.

In the mid-1800s a material called gutta-percha, a gum harvested from a Malaysian tree, was introduced into common use in Europe. It was used for waterproofing undersea telegraph cables and other purposes, including making the first decent all-weather golf ball. To make the ball, the gutta-percha was heated and rolled into a solid ball by hand. With increased mechanization and industrialization, the balls were cast in molds by machine.

The balls, smooth when new, sometimes broke into pieces, and did not travel as well as the featheries. Interestingly enough, as the balls were played more, they flew better. It appears that the rougher surface that came with repeated play made a difference in travel distance.

This is the first clue to why modern golf balls have dimples. A British scientist named Tait is credited with the first serious academic study of the aerodynamics of the golf ball. He held the chair of Natural Philosophy at Edinburgh University in Scotland (natural philosophy being the term used then for physics), and an avid golfer.

He discovered that when a ball moves through the air at a good clip, it creates a zone of turbulence behind it that drags on the ball. Dimples, as it turns out, decrease the zone of turbulence and reduce the drag on the ball. The benefit of spin is that it forces the turbulent wake down and away from the ball (back toward the driver, if done right), and the opposite effect is felt by the ball (it goes up and away from the driver). See sidebar "Diving for Balls."

THE KODIAK OPEN

Kodiak Island, off the southern coast of Alaska, is largely inhabited by fishermen and -women and their families. It is a rough environment to work and play in, and it seems only appropriate that when the locals play, they play games that reflect the kind of people they are.

The Pillar Mountain Golf Classic is played on Kodiak every March over two days, and consists of a single hole, par 70. The tee is located in the heart of town, with the cup being at the top of Pillar Mountain, fourteen hundred feet above the community. The cup is a five-gallon bucket embedded in the snow at the mountain's peak. Players note that while this might seem like a large target, putting in the snow is exceedingly difficult.

> • **In parts of the Middle East, where grass and the water to grow it are rare, some golfers play sand courses, carrying a bit of AstroTurf or carpet with them to shoot from.**

Standard golf clubs are allowed, but it is recommended that you also bring orange balls (much of the course is played on snow), warm clothes, brush-cutting tools for the alder thickets, a spotter and caddy to assist in finding balls, and a noise maker to warn bears of your approach.

Entry is open, requiring a $50 fee. The official rules, paraphrased here rather than quoted so we don't get sued, are:

- Balls must be played where they lie; a lost ball costs you a two-stroke penalty. If a ball is in a totally unplayable lie, it can be moved five club lengths—and no closer to the hole—at the cost of a one-stroke penalty.
- A ball buried in snow (and therefore unplayable) is considered a lost ball with a one-stroke penalty, and may be moved as above.
- You can't use two-way radios, dogs, or tracking devices to find your balls.

- No chainsaws or other power saws. You can use handsaws and hatchets to clear brush.
- A golfer may bring one caddie and one spotter. At least one person in the trio must be twenty-one years of age.
- Dress *appropriately!* You get hypothermia, it's your problem.
- No swearing at the golf officials—you'll get hit with a $25 fine.
- Cart off your own trash, including cigarette butts. Leaving your trash can get you disqualified.
- Do not disturb the bears. It'll cost you a five-stroke penalty "unless you get away, then we'll subtract ten strokes!"

ICE GOLFING

If you're up for some seriously manly golfing, check out the World Ice Golf Championship in Uummannaq, Greenland. Golfers compete over two days (thirty-six holes in total) on a course set out on a frozen fjord near the town. Sand traps and water hazards are not problems, but the course does feature icebergs and large Arctic animals.

Because of the conditions, each hole is about 25 percent shorter than those in more moderate climates (golf balls do not perform nearly as well in the cold weather as under other conditions), and the holes themselves are twice the diameter of standard holes. The course boundaries and the centerline are marked with colored poles every fifty meters. The boundaries are also shoveled clear of snow, as is the "green," which is painted red to improve visibility. Players are required to clean up any tracks they leave on the green with a broom.

The rules of the game are in accordance with the current international rules for golf with a few exceptions: any ball that has a bad lie may be lifted, cleaned, and relocated within fifteen centimeters of its original position (though not closer to the hole); any ball played on the fairway must be teed, and once teed is in play; golf carts and buggies are not allowed. This is sensible, given the likelihood the carts would just freeze up on the ice.

If you want to enter this tournament, some advice: Use steel shaft clubs—they perform well in temperatures that are typically below 10°F. In place of the traditional khakis and polo shirt, layers of clothing are recommended, including long or thermal underwear, snow pants, long-neck top, parka, hat, and a bala-clava (a full-head hood with an opening for the face, favored by serious skiers, bank robbers, and SWAT teams), and if it gets really cold, scarf, snow goggles, gloves, and appropriate footwear. Heated socks are a must. Obviously, this extra clothing encumbers optimal performance, which is part of the reason the holes are shorter than standard.

A handicap below 36 is required to be eligible for the tournament.

DIVING FOR BALLS

The exact number of golf balls chipped, driven, or sliced into water hazards every year is anybody's guess, but the number is a whole lot bigger than Shaq's annual payout from the Lakers, and his shoe and taco endorsements combined. Call it "substantial." In many cases the balls are retrieved, in the most obvious way, by wading or from boats with scoops and nets. The extreme end is ball diving.

Most ball divers use traditional scuba gear, with a single tank, and suit appropriate for the water temperatures. The waters are usually shallow, and a diver can stay down for over an hour, which is usually adequate to fill the commercial laundry bags that are used for collection. On a good day, the divers just shovel the balls into the bags, and hauls in excess of five thousand balls a day are not uncommon.

Interestingly enough, most golf ball divers pay for the right to harvest the balls, which they then resell to driving ranges, pro shops, and others for around ten cents a ball. This is not universally true, and some courses contract with pro-fessional diving services or dive clubs to clean up the water on the courses (including bottles, cans, clubs, trash, golf carts, lawn mowers, and miscella-neous golf gear).

It isn't a dangerous job, under normal circumstances, though it can be. Scuba diving is risky anytime, and when the diving is done at altitude (above three thousand feet), the risks increase. Sometimes the water is a hazard in itself, either due to cold or, worse, due to where the water comes from. In some drier states, the water may be "reclaimed," which means it's chemically treated sewage. Some courses, such as those in the southeastern United States, feature alligators as part of the natural hazards, in which case diving for balls is not advised.

ENTERTAINMENT

Real guys boycott the Oscars, the Grammys, the Emmys, and all the rest of the self-congratulatory award shows. The failure of the Academy and their lackeys to recognize the genius that was the Three Stooges is further proof of the feminist agenda in Hollywood (where any tear-jerking, cross-dressing chick flick is almost assured of an award).

NYUCK NYUCK NYUCK—THE THREE STOOGES

Stooges. Women hate them. Men love them. It's not possible to explain the why's and how's, so best just to accept the fact and move on.

Contrary to the group's name, there were actually a total of six Stooges: Moe, Larry, Curly, Shemp, Joe, and Curly-Joe. Moe, Curly, and Shemp were brothers (Harry Moses Horwitz, Jerome Horwitz, and Samuel Horwitz respectively, though they went by the last name of Howard). Larry, whose real name was Louis Feinberg, Joe (Joseph Besser) who replaced Shemp at the time of his death in 1955, and Curly-Joe DeRita (Joseph Wardell), who joined the Stooge's briefly when Joe left to care for his sick wife, were all unrelated.

The Stooges started in 1922, and there were just two, Moe and Shemp, who worked as junior partners in a comedy routine with Ted Healy. They had an on-and-off partnership, adding Larry to the act in 1925. Larry left for two years (1927–1929), but otherwise he was one of two permanent Stooges (Moe Howard being the other). Shemp rejoined and left the act several times, leaving before Curly arrived and returning after Curly's death in 1946.

In 1934 the youngest Howard brother (and in the opinion of many, the finest Stooge ever) joined the act as Curly. Jerome Howard, also known as "Babe" to his family, joined Moe and Larry when Shemp went solo. His distinctive haircut, the shaved head, was thought up to make Curly seem less ordinary, and somehow it fit in with the bad hair of Moe and Larry. Jerome Howard actually had very thick hair and a mustache before joining the team.

- **Moe was married to Harry Houdini's cousin, Helen Schonberger.**
- **Shemp died in a cab after watching a boxing match.**
- **Moe made four movies on his own: *Space Master X-7, Doctor Death, Seeker of Souls, Don't Worry, We'll Think of a Title,* and *Senior Prom* (as the associate producer).**
- **Larry was both a violin player and a successful lightweight boxer.**

Curly was famous for his ad-libbing (to counter a bad memory for his lines) and physical comedy. He was also quite the lady's man: he had married four times by the time of his death at age forty-eight.

LAND OF THE *KAIJU—GOJIRA*

Godzilla, or "Gojira" as he is properly known in Japan, is an anachronism in the world of film. While Hollywood moviemakers seek to improve the quality of their special effects through sophisticated computer programs, Toho Films in Japan has been content for nearly fifty years to make use of a man in a rubber suit and painfully detailed scale models of Japanese cities and countryside (all of which are stepped on, burnt down, blown up, or otherwise destroyed during filming).

The first Godzilla movie was made in 1954 and released in Japan under the name *Gojira*, which is an artificial word, combining the Japanese words for gorilla and whale. Since then, the original *kaiju* (Japanese for monster) has appeared in twenty-three feature films.

The movie *Gojira* has never been seen by American audiences in its original form. Instead it was taken and recut with new footage filmed with American actors, featuring Raymond Burr (well known from the television shows *Perry Mason* and *Ironside*) as reporter Steve Martin. When a new version was made in the 1980s, also featuring Burr, he was never referred to as "Steve Martin," in fear that people would make a connection to the comedian of the same name, reducing his credibility as a serious character.

With the exception of the Hollywood version of *Godzilla* released in 1999, every Godzilla movie ever made always had the monster (and many of the other *kaiju* in the movie) played by a man wearing a rubber suit. The first suit was manufactured from latex rubber, and was modeled on the T-Rex and the stegosaurus to produce a bipedal dragon with armored plates on his back. When complete, the suit weighed over one hundred pounds.

At the time the first movie was made, there were only two effects available to achieve the look: stop-motion animation using models, and the man in the rubber suit. Stop-motion animation, raised to a high art by Ray Harryhausen, was the high tech of the day, but prohibitively expensive. Thus the rubber suit.

> • Godzilla's win-loss-tie record in on-screen movie fights is 28-9-12.
> • Godzilla's "voice" was produced by detuning a string on a bass cello and drawing a bow across it slowly.

Six different actors played Godzilla over the years, each one bringing a particular look and feel to the character. Godzilla aficionados claim to be able to distinguish among them based on their movements.

BOND. JAMES BOND.

The James Bond character was developed by Ian Fleming, who himself had been employed by the intelligence and espionage arms of the British military during the Second World War. Many of the familiar movies in the Bond series are taken from Fleming's books. Bond is reported to be the most recognizable fictional character in the world today.

The Bond stories and movies introduced the public to villains such as Blofeld (played by Donald Pleasence in *You Only Live Twice;* Telly Savalas in *On Her Majesty's Secret Service;* and Charles Gray, who also played the Noted Criminologist in *The Rocky Horror Picture Show,* in *Diamonds Are Forever*), Auric Goldfinger, Oddjob, and Dr. No. It also gave us female leads such as Octopussy, Bibi Dahl, Holly Goodhead, Plenty O'Toole, and Pussy Galore.

James Bond has been played by five actors (so far), only one of whom was born in England.

- Sean Connery was in seven Bond films, including the only one not produced by Albert "Cubby" Broccoli (*Never Say Never Again*). He is Scottish and got early acting experience in the chorus in a stage production of *South Pacific* after leaving the British Army due to stomach problems.
- George Lazenby, one film. Ego problems were cited. Born in Australia.

- Roger Moore, seven films. Born in England. Also starred in the television series *The Saint*.
- Timothy Dalton, two films. Born in Wales.
- Pierce Brosnan. The current Bond, Brosnan has done four films to date. He was born in Ireland.

BOND

The Bond movies, in order, are (with the actor starring as Bond in parentheses)

Dr. No (Sean Connery)

From Russia with Love (Sean Connery)

Goldfinger (Sean Connery)

Thunderball (Sean Connery)

You Only Live Twice (Sean Connery)

On Her Majesty's Secret Service (George Lazenby)

Diamonds Are Forever (Sean Connery)

Live and Let Die (Roger Moore)

The Man with the Golden Gun (Roger Moore)

The Spy Who Loved Me (Roger Moore)

Moonraker (Roger Moore)

For Your Eyes Only (Roger Moore)

Octopussy (Roger Moore)

Never Say Never Again (Sean Connery)

A View to a Kill (Roger Moore)

The Living Daylights (Timothy Dalton)

Licence to Kill (Timothy Dalton)

GoldenEye (Pierce Brosnan)

Tomorrow Never Dies (Pierce Brosnan)

The World Is Not Enough (Pierce Brosnan)

Die Another Day (Pierce Brosnan)

HOW TO PLAY BACCARAT

Baccarat is Bond's game of choice. It originated in Italy and France, and the name means "zero."

Eight decks of cards are shuffled together and placed in a shoe (a wooden box with a slot for the cards to be drawn at one end). The player and the bank each get two cards facedown. The player's cards are exposed, then the bank's. Face cards and tens have a value of zero (hence the name). An ace counts as one. A total of nine or eight with just two cards is called a natural. A nine wins automatically, followed by eight if no player or the bank has a nine.

Players bet against the bank, and others at the table bet on the bank, the player, or a tie (ties pay off at eight to one odds).

A player must draw a third card if his hand totals one to five, or ten. Drawing six or seven, the player must stand. If the player draws an eight or nine on the first two cards, he must stand and the banker cannot draw beyond his first two cards.

BUGS BUNNY AND WARNER BROS. CARTOONS

Bugs Bunny is probably one of the most recognizable cartoon characters in the world, though Disney might debate whether Mickey Mouse has that honor or not. The primary distinction between them, after their species and studio, is probably one of attitude. Bugs is rather offbeat and irreverent. It has been reported that his character was inspired by Groucho Marx.

A select group of guys deserves the credit for the toons:

> Tex Avery: Fred "Tex" Avery worked at Warner Brothers from 1935 until 1942, and is considered responsible for introducing an offbeat, "wise guy" attitude to the

company's cartoons. He introduced Daffy Duck in 1937, and directed a cartoon called "Wild Hare," the cartoon most people consider the first real Bugs Bunny cartoon.

MEL BLANC: Mel Blanc worked at Warner Brothers from 1937 until his death in 1989 as the voice of such characters as Bugs Bunny, Porky Pig, Daffy Duck, Foghorn Leghorn, Marvin the Martian, Yosemite Sam, Tweety, Sylvester, and Pepe Le Pew, among others. After his death his son continued providing voice talents for many Warner Brothers cartoons.

FRITZ FRELENG: Isadore "Fritz" Freleng started his animation career at Disney, but joined Warner Brothers in 1930. He specialized in musical cartoons, and created the characters of Porky Pig and Yosemite Sam.

BOB CLAMPETT: Clampett created the characters of Tweety, Beaky Buzzard, Gremlins, and the Do-Do.

CHUCK JONES: Chuck Jones worked at Warner Brothers under the direction of Tex Avery, and worked on the earliest Porky Pig cartoons. He was instrumental in developing the characters of Bugs Bunny, Elmer Fudd, and Daffy Duck, and creating Road Runner, Wile E. Coyote, Pepe Le Pew, Michigan J. Frog, and Marvin the Martian. He also directed the famous animated version of Dr. Suess's *How the Grinch Stole Christmas*.

ROBERT MCKIMSON: He created the Tasmanian Devil and Foghorn Leghorn, and worked on the development of many of the most famous characters, including Bugs Bunny, Daffy Duck, Porky Pig, Speedy Gonzalez, and Sylvester.

BOWEL AND BLADDER

Guys spend about thirty minutes each and every day—one-forty-eighth of our life—camped out on the crapper. I don't care *what* you're doing there. The fact is, your hairy butt is planted, and the older you get, the longer you're gonna spend there. Given that, it's high time you use this dead space in your life productively and get some *mental* exercise for a change.

The Bowel

AIRPLANE RESTROOMS

The toilet in your bathroom (unless you live in a yurt in some plumbing-free Third World hellhole) works using a passive siphon. Flushing causes the water level in the bowl to rise. At the bottom of the bowl, a molded channel called the siphon rises up to slightly above the level of water in the bowl when it is at rest, then drops down to floor level, connecting to the waste pipe.

When the toilet is flushed, water level rises in the bowl. Some of it enters at the rim to rinse the bowl, but the majority comes out toward the bottom of the bowl through a hole called the siphon jet. The siphon jet accelerates the water and waste out, creating the siphon effect.

This does not work on an airplane. Planes bounce around, meaning a water-filled bowl would be dumping water all over the place in bumpy air. Instead of a siphon, they use a vacuum effect to clean the bowl. When an airplane toilet is flushed, a small quantity of chemically treated water is sprayed from a reservoir into the bowl to clean it, while the drain line is opened. The drain line is a vacuum, and it draws the waste material and liquid off to a holding tank. Toilets of this type use very little water or liquid, usually less than a half gallon as compared to the average home toilet that usually requires over two gallons to flush properly.

On an airplane the waste material is sucked into a holding tank for later removal and disposal once the plane has landed at a properly equipped airport. Contrary to popular belief, airlines are not ejecting killer blocks of frozen excrement in the skies over Kansas—not on purpose, anyway.

Vacuum toilets have many advantages over siphon-water toilets beyond low water consumption. Because of their design, their drain lines can run in any direction, including straight up.

- **The toilets in the Forbidden City in China consist of several small six-inch metal gratings on the floor leading to a cesspit or drain. Toilet tissue is not typically provided.**
- **In China, being connected to the World Wide Web is more common than having a flush toilet.**
- **In Singapore, it is illegal not to flush a toilet.**
- **The origin of the word "toilet" comes from the French, *toilette*, meaning the act of washing, dressing, and preparing oneself.**
- **During takeoff, landing, and space walks, astronauts wear diapers to catch their waste. This was also the norm in the early days of space flight, when the trips were short (and bathrooms were not provided on the spacecraft).**

TOILETS IN SPACE—HOW DO ASTRONAUTS DO IT?

While you never see a toilet in *Star Trek* or *Star Wars,* the issue of voiding one's bowels in space is important and complex, especially given the lack of rest stops.

Space toilets are not dissimilar in configuration to the kind found on campers or boats, with a few differences. For starters, terrestrial toilets count on gravity, and use water as the primary means of motivating the waste material. This presents two significant problems when placing a toilet in space. Water isn't light at eight pounds per gallon, and if a toilet requires one gallon per flush, a significant amount of water would need to be available for an extended space mission. The design and operation of spacecraft are such that severe restrictions on excess weight are necessary.

The most serious problem, however, is the lack of gravity. Once fecal matter has been forced from the body, it becomes a free-floating body in orbit, presenting unpleasant consequences if it is not quickly contained. To counteract this, space toilets take advantage of air pressure differentials. Simply speaking, they vacuum up the waste material.

Urination is accomplished by fitting a small cup or receptacle to the head of the penis or over the urethra, tight enough to prevent seepage, and letting nature and a little negative air pressure handle the rest. Defecation is much the same, though one uses a toilet, of course. In both cases, the waste is taken off to a storage container. Excess air is removed and reused for future movements.

Whether standing or seated, the other major challenge in using a commode in space is staying in place at the toilet, and not floating away. Since the space toilet uses a cup attachment for urination and the cup is usable by male or female astronauts, spacefarers of either gender can use it standing up, slipping their feet under a toe bar. If taking a seat is required, there are Velcro-equipped footholds, bars that put pressure on the thighs to hold the astronaut down, and handholds for an added degree of stabilization.

NASA does not haul water for waste disposal into space, but at the end of shuttle missions, the astronauts bring the fecal matter back for disposal on earth. If the fecal matter were dumped into space, it would represent a safety risk to future space missions, given that it would be orbiting at a high rate of speed and could do significant damage were it to strike a satellite or spaceship. It would be really bad PR to report that the billion-dollar Hubble Space Telescope was taken out by five pounds of ka-ka moving at seventeen thousand miles per hour.

TOILET PAPER

Toilet *paper* cannot have been available before there was paper, which has been available only since the eighth century. Even then, the value of paper was such that it is unlikely it would ever have been put into common, widespread use for purposes of hygiene. The first recorded case of paper being used in this manner was by the Bureau of Imperial Supplies in China, which began producing paper in A.D. 1391 for the emperor. The paper was made in sheets measuring 24 x 36 inches.

Before the introduction of purpose-made tissue or paper, people made do with what was at hand, so to speak: newspaper and catalogue pages were used in Western countries in more recent times, but a variety of other methods have been identified:

- During the Middle Ages, "gompf" sticks (a kind of scraper) were used, as were hay, grass, and leaves.
- The Vikings used discarded wool.
- Ancient Romans used a sponge soaked in salt water, fixed to the end of a short stick, or wool and rose water.
- French royalty used lace or hemp.
- Eskimos used moss and snow.

It was not until paper began to be mass produced in large, cheap quantities that it was introduced commercially for this use. A New Yorker produced packaged toilet tissue for sale in 1857, and in 1880 the British Perforated Paper Company began selling boxes of precut paper for bathroom use. The Scott Paper Company introduced rolled toilet paper in 1890.

FLATULENCE

Flatulence is part of the animal condition. It is simply the body's way of getting rid of excess gasses through a convenient opening. Most humans do this six to twenty times per day, venting up to two thousand milliliters of gas (enough to fill two good-sized pop bottles).

The gasses come from swallowed air, diffusion from the blood, and production within the gut (the major source). Bacteria in the bowels help digest food, and as they do so, they produce gasses, most notably hydrogen, carbon dioxide, and methane. Other gasses include nitrogen and oxygen. Chemically speaking, carbohydrates and fiber (foods such as beans, cabbage, and mushrooms) will cause the body to produce the most gas.

- **Flatulence in foreign languages:**

    German: Blahung

    Hebrew: נאד (pronounced "nod")

    Russian: напыщенность (pronounced "napyschonnost")

    Hungarian: Σζ Γλσζορυλ)σ

    Japanese: Kochou

    Italian: Flatulenza

    French: Flatulence

    Italian: Flatulenza

    Spanish: Flatulencia

- **Many cultures believe that belching is manly or good manners, indicated a meal was well received. In parts of the Middle East and Southeast Asia, a belch will often be accompanied by saying "*Alhamdulillah*," meaning "Praise be to God," as a sign of thanks for the meal.**

Vegetarians produce more gas than meat eaters. The bacteria in the human colon thrive on the cellulose found in the cell walls of most vegetables, and produce significantly more gas from its decomposition. Diets high in fats and protein cause less gas production.

In terms of aroma, the unpleasant smells associated with flatulence are caused by sulfurous byproducts. But not everyone produces these—only about one in three people.

Only 30 percent of the population produces an adequate amount of methane content in their gas for it to be ignited.

The Bladder

URINALS

The urinal is a logical extension of the male capability and propensity to pee standing up. As often is remarked, any place a man can unzip can be considered a good spot to go, and the invention of the urinal is simply a logical step if one wishes to either capture the urine or carry it away.

Urinals come in all sizes, shapes, and configurations, from the single-user kind commonly found in modern public restrooms (though rarely in private homes) to a nearly three-hundred-foot-long urinal temporarily erected in New York at the base of the Verrazano Narrows Bridge at the starting line of the New York Marathon.

- **Urine has an economic value. Urine contains acids that are useful in some activities, such as leather tanning, and there are archeological and historical records to indicate that it has been used in this particular industry for hundreds of years.**
- **In March of 1866, American Andrew Rankin received a patent for the urinal.**
- **It is a little-known fact that if a urinal cake is placed in a pint of certain beers or lagers, it will sink and float repeatedly until it is fully dissolved. (Note: Please feel free to experiment with different beers—but for the love of Pete, don't drink it afterward!)**

The urinal is normally associated with men's toilet facilities, though various attempts have been made to enable women to pee standing up or to use something similar to the men's version of the urinal. A device known as the Urinette Sheinal was introduced by a Pensacola, Florida, woman in the early 1990s. It had a tube connected to a cup, with the tube feeding into the base of a wall-mounted ceramic fixture similar in shape and function to the more traditional male model. The cup was held over the urethra, and the woman peed as normal, except she could do so while standing.

The Urinette Sheinal never caught on.

URINAL CAKES

The active ingredient in urine cakes is paradichlorobenzene, a white solid crystal with a wet oily surface. It is volatile and gives off an odor not unlike that produced by mothballs (which are often made of naphthalene). Paradichlorobenzene is sometimes used to make mothballs and moth crystals, but is most commonly found (outside of the urine cake) in diaper, toilet, and room deodorizers.

As a health risk, paradichlorobenzene may cause some problems. Excessive inhalation can lead to headaches, eye irritation, congestion, loss of appetite, nausea, and vomiting. Prolonged contact can result in allergic reactions, and ingestion may cause liver and kidney damage, and a condition known as methemoglobianemia (which interferes with the uptake of oxygen). The lesson here, guys, is you shouldn't take any longer than you need. Drain it, zip it, and move along!

URINAL USE DISCOMFORT

Almost every guy hates taking a leak right up close and personal with another guy—it's why we always leave a one-urinal no-fly zone between us and the guy to either side (when we can). But hey, it's not that we're sissies. We've got a condition: *avoidant paruresis,* more commonly known as shy bladder. At least 7 percent of the population suffers from this. It's a type of anxiety disorder, making the act of urinating almost impossible—the muscles just won't relax enough to let you go. The good news is you can be cured. Scientific behavior modification techniques are available, but in extreme cases you may require catheterization.

THE GREAT OUTDOORS

Your ancestors, the guys of old, were comfortable in the wilderness. They crossed oceans, climbed unnamed mountain ranges, swam rivers, and lived off tree bark and beaver entrails. They were tough hombres, dealing with fleas and lice, making their own clothes out of buckskin, living by their wits. When you're out in the great outdoors, sitting on a titanium campstool in your Gore-Tex coat, making an espresso on the Primus stove, you can reflect on the information in this chapter, and be grateful you're not one of your ancestors.

Things You Didn't Know You Could (or Shouldn't) Eat and Other Helpful Survival Hints

PLANTS YOU SHOULD AVOID

When camping, hiking, or in an emergency situation, there is a wide range of plant matter that can be eaten, either to supplement the diet or for purposes of survival. These include various nuts, berries, tubers, and foliage. There are many plants, however, which are exceedingly dangerous and should be avoided at all costs.

> DAFFODIL, NARCISSUS, AND HYACINTH BULBS: These will make you very sick and may kill you.
>
> OLEANDER LEAVES AND BRANCHES: Extremely poisonous, these affect the heart. Avoid cooking food over oleander wood.
>
> RHUBARB LEAVES: Fatal if ingested.
>
> LILY OF THE VALLEY: The leaves and flowers will cause an irregular heartbeat.
>
> FOXGLOVE LEAVES: Causes irregular heartbeat.
>
> WISTERIA: The seeds and seed pods cause severe gastrointestinal upset and can kill.
>
> LAURELS, AZALEAS, AND RHODODENDRONS: No parts of these plants can safely be eaten.

- The rule of thumb for eating wild berries is based on color. Blue-colored berries are almost always safe to eat. White berries are almost always poisonous. Red-colored berries can be either. As always, exercise caution and judgment and know the fruit before you eat it.

CHERRIES: The twigs and foliage of cherry trees contain a compound that releases cyanide.

OAK: Acorns and foliage will damage your kidneys.

POISON HEMLOCK: Though it looks like a carrot, consumption of any part is fatal.

TIDBITS AND USEFUL BITS FROM THE *SAS SURVIVAL HANDBOOK*

One of the standards of the Special Air Services (SAS) is the survival kit, a collection of items that are essential in a crisis. It's been tested and proven in terrible conditions, and yet is small enough to fit into a coat pocket. The recommended container is a two-ounce tobacco tin.

The tin is polished on the inside of the lid to make a mirrorlike reflecting surface, making it useful as a signaling device. Once this is done, the essentials are packed in and padded with cotton to protect the contents and prevent it from rattling in a combat environment—and for purposes of fire-starting or medical needs. Here are the recommended contents:

- Standard, strike-anywhere matches, dipped in wax to make them waterproof.
- One square candle made of tallow which can be eaten for energy in a crisis or used for frying food.
- Flint and steel to make sparks, no matter how wet it is.
- Magnifying glass for starting a fire in direct sunlight, as well as for removing insect stingers or splinters.
- Needles and thread, including one needle large enough to be threaded with coarse thread or animal sinew. Include strong thread and coil it around the needles to save space.
- A selection of fishhooks, lines, and weights. Bring as much line as possible. Hooks can be used to catch fish or birds.
- Luminous compass, preferably liquid-filled.
- Beta light: beta lights are small, coin-sized lights using light-emitting crystals or diodes.
- Two to four feet of brass wire.
- Wooden-handled flexible saw.
- Medical kit: Pack all medications in watertight, airtight containers. Bring analgesics, intestinal sedatives, antibiotics, antihistamines, water sterilizing tablets, antimalarial drugs, potassium permanganate (sterilizes water and is an excellent antifungal

medication), two to three scalpel blades, butterfly sutures, small bandages, and one to two unlubricated, heavy-duty condoms (really, these are very useful for keeping batteries dry, carrying water—up to two pints—and covering wounds on the fingers).

Once packed, the tin should be sealed with waterproof tape. The tape must be easily removed and replaced. The packing date should be written on the tin so the age of the contents is known, and older items should be replaced regularly.

ORIGIN OF THE BOY SCOUTS

The Boy Scouts of America trace their roots back to 1907 and Lord Robert Baden-Powell. Baden-Powell was a British soldier, serving in India and Africa. During the Boer War, he commanded the defense of Mafikeng. He formed the South African Constabulary, and formed the Boy Scouts as a means of teaching young men and boys the essentials of self-sufficiency, outdoor skills, and basic moral fiber. For his efforts, he was awarded a peerage in 1929. In its early days scouting in America was sponsored by the Young Men's Christian Association (YMCA), but in 1910, a Chicago publisher, William Dickson Boyce, incorporated the Boy Scouts of America.

Worldwide, scouting is estimated to include twenty-five million scouts, most between eleven and eighteen years of age.

Poisonous Critters

TOXINS—THE MOST LETHAL BITES THERE ARE

There are four primary types of toxins used by animals. They are neurotoxins, cardioactive toxins, hemotoxins, and myotoxins. They attack, respectively, the nervous system, heart, blood system, and muscles. Puffer fish, cone shells, the blue-ringed octopus, and the Portuguese man-of-war all inject neurotoxin, whereas the box jellyfish (also known as the "sea wasp" and common to the seas around Australia) produces a myotoxin. The box jellyfish is reported to be the most venomous animal on earth.

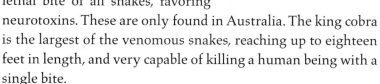

SNAKES: Venomous snakes are found on all continents other than Antarctica. The taipan, also known as the "fierce snake," has the most lethal bite of all snakes, favoring neurotoxins. These are only found in Australia. The king cobra is the largest of the venomous snakes, reaching up to eighteen feet in length, and very capable of killing a human being with a single bite.

In the Americas, the western diamondback rattlesnake is the most dangerous snake. They kill more people than any other American snake. They are of the neurotoxin school of venoms, and about 10 percent of their victims die.

SPIDERS: For their size and body mass, spiders are one of the most dangerous members of the animal kingdom. In the Americas, the most commonly known is the black widow. Found in dark and quiet areas, the females are exceedingly toxic, but deaths are rare due to the relatively small volume of toxin they can inject (compared to a snake). Black widows also have the distinction of being cannibalistic, with the female eating the male after mating (this is not a unique behavior among spiders and insects). Their offspring are cannabalistic as well. Upon hatching, they will prey on each other until only a few remain.

While the black widow is one of the better-known poisonous spiders, the range of dangerous spiders in the New World includes the brown recluse and the hobo (also known as the "aggressive house spider"). And where widows are fairly shy, the hobo is aggressive and will bite with little provocation.

The most dangerous member of the spider community is the Sydney funnel web spider (another product of Australia). Frequently lethal to human beings, they combine good size (two to three inches) with nasty fangs that are reported to be able to penetrate a human fingernail, and have an aggressive disposition. Most spiders will skitter away from a human. Not so with the funnel web. A funnel web will rear up and threaten a human or other animal.

Lizards: Lizards are a relatively low-risk group in terms of venom and toxicity. Only the Gila monster and the Mexican beaded lizard are known to be venomous, and fortunately they are only found in limited ranges of the American southwest and parts of Mexico. What's more, they spend the bulk of their time dormant and are not commonly encountered by humans. Their bites are not universally lethal, but serious enough to kill a small child.

Author's Choice—Komodo Dragons: Reptiles and lizards are not a particularly terrifying group of animals as a group.

Ever since dinosaurs ceased to rule the earth, and ignoring alligators and crocodiles, the lizards and reptiles of the world haven't really been much of a threat—other than snakes, of course, and the resident of a small, desolate island east of Bali.

The Komodo dragon is native to the island of Komodo and five or so adjacent islands—fortunately. They are the largest species of lizard alive today, up to ten feet in length and *five hundred pounds!*

Komodos hunt in two ways. For smaller prey, it's a matter of stalk, run down, rip and tear. They sometimes hunt in groups and will go after deer, pigs, goats, buffalo, humans, and even each other. In spite of bad eyesight and poor hearing, they are vicious hunters (an extraordinary sense of smell makes up for the less sensitive nature of their other senses). They swim, run, dig, and climb, and they have a mouth loaded with very sharp teeth.

The Komodo does not shy from attacking very large animals (such as cattle), in spite of the size difference. The Komodo's mouth harbors masses of septic bacteria. When hunting larger prey, the Komodo will bite the animal, leaving a wound filled with the bugs. In a few hours the bacteria multiply rapidly and poison the prey enough to kill it or slow it down

- A license is required to hunt wild diamondbacks, though this is not the case if one chooses to keep one as a pet.
- Snakes do not urinate.
- Bee stings kill more people in the United States than snakebites.
- The top phobia of Americans surveyed is snakes, followed by being buried alive.
- The largest spider is the goliath bird-eating spider, with a legspan of almost twelve inches.
- On the plus side, many scientists use the effects of animal venom to research and produce new drugs. Lizard venom is being researched toward a treatment of diabetes—somehow the venom helps improve the production of insulin.

significantly. (The stink of the infection also helps the Komodo track the victim, as well as attracting other dragons.)

As a result of this hunting method, the Komodo often begins eating while the victim is still alive.

MOSQUITOES

There are about twenty-seven hundred different species of mosquito identified by science to date. Of these, only about a hundred species can carry disease. Those that do are particularly dangerous to humans, carrying such diseases as malaria, encephalitis, dengue fever, and yellow fever. In most cases, the carriers are the females of the species, as most male mosquitoes drink the juices of fruit and plants instead of blood.

Mosquitoes track their prey at distances up to one hundred feet. They respond to the smells of warm-blooded animals, particularly carbon dioxide, ammonia, and water vapor, and are sensitive to heat as well.

Mosquitoes can be combated by either repelling them or killing them. Repellents include DEET, permethrin, and citronella. Bug zappers can be used to kill the insects, but are indiscriminate and kill many less noxious insects, such as moths. Other methods of eliminating or controlling mosquitoes include removing or poisoning their breeding grounds (stagnant water), though this too may affect animals and 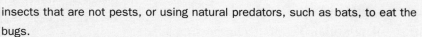 insects that are not pests, or using natural predators, such as bats, to eat the bugs.

Avoiding mosquitoes may be the most sane and sensible way of dealing with them. Mosquitoes are most active at dusk and dawn. They also avoid being out-of-doors during the heat of the day as it tends to dry them out. Mosquitoes can't fly well in a stiff breeze, so windy days are good for avoiding being bitten.

JUST PLAIN WEIRD AND A LITTLE MORBID

In the community of guys, the standard measure of the quality of a bit of information will always be whether or not you can get another guy to spray beer out his nose when you hit him with it. With these, you should be able to get beer *and* pretzels. (And man, that stings!)

Weird Eats

BUG EATING

For residents of North America or Western Europe (with the exception of parts of France), the idea of eating a bug may be nauseating. Much of this is based on objections to both the nature of the food and associations with disease and filth. However, the high percentage of processed foods consumed by Americans and the manner in which the foods are processed results in a small but definite amount of insect parts being included. It is estimated that the average American or European will inadvertently and unknowingly consume at least one pound of insects in their lifetime with no adverse effects.

By contrast, in much of the rest of the world, bugs—or more accurately, insects—represent an important dietary supplement, providing good sources of protein and fats. Some are even considered a delicacy.

Putting cultural and perceptual issues aside, there are many good reasons for eating bugs as healthy alternatives to more traditional foods. For example, 100 grams of ground beef have almost 300 calories and over 21 grams of fat, whereas the same weight of crickets has 121 calories and only 5.5 grams of fat. Advocates of the practice of eating insects, called entomophagy, point out many other benefits.

- Insects taste very good. They can be prepared and eaten in any number of ways—raw to boiled, fried to baked—and can also be mixed into many already popular dishes.
- Unlike most food animals or crops, insects are easy and simple to raise. They do not require acres of pasture or farmland to provide a modest crop, and there are no stalls to muck out, no bales of hay to lug around, and no veterinarian bills. Many insects can be fed on the same material that might otherwise be thrown in the trash or a compost heap.
- No animal rights groups have taken up the cause of the insect, and most people have no ethical dilemma about "slaughtering" a bug.
- Insects are plentiful. Pound for pound, insects outnumber and outweigh all other Earth species *combined*.
- Unlike cattle or other range animals, forests and wildlife habitats are not threatened by the raising of insect crops.

At least fourteen hundred insect species have been identified as safe to consume, and with the millions of species of insects that exist, there are probably thousands more to choose from. The biggest problem an insect consumer may encounter is finding a convenient source to buy them in adequate quantities. Occasionally an insect food product is made available for sale, but usually only as a novelty item. Except in those areas of the world where the practice is acceptable, insects aren't generally found in grocery store or market stalls.

Fortunately, there are other good sources of insects available if one knows where to look. Almost any hunting, fishing, or bait shop will have a good supply of worms and crickets, and most pet stores can provide mealy worms. There are also insect suppliers to be found on the Internet.

In a rural setting, insects can be collected from the surrounding land, though this is a somewhat labor-intensive undertaking. Doing this in an urbanized environment or around croplands that are sprayed with insecticides is highly risky, due to the potential of ingesting these toxins.

The insect eater also has the option of raising them himself, which is a very simple undertaking once a rootstock is in hand. A terrarium fitted with a tight, screened lid and newspaper or wood chips can be used as an effective breeding ground for many species, providing them with an appropriate food source. Be aware, though, that just as with many other foods, what the insects are fed will affect their flavor.

INSECT RECIPES

Insects may be prepared and eaten as an entrée, side dish, or as an ingredient in other foods. They may be cooked in any number of ways, including fried, baked, and boiled, or as with sashimi, they may be eaten raw.

- For beginners, it is recommended to mix insects with other, more familiar foods. Mealworms, for example, can be oven-dried on a cookie sheet and then ground in an herb grinder, coffee grinder, or food processor. The resulting powder is a good substitute for flour in oatmeal or chocolate chip cookie recipes. Use about one-quarter to one-half cup of mealworm powder to replace an equal amount of wheat flour.

- Try adding one to one and a half cups of crickets to a cheesecake. The crickets should be dry-roasted and only their abdomens should be used. Remove heads, antennae, and legs.
- As for entrées, try deep-fried water beetles. These are breaded with a tempura batter and panko bread crumbs to make them crispy, then fried in heated oil in a wok for about sixty seconds. Served with vegetables and the dipping sauce of choice, they are crispy and very flavorful.
- Mealworms may be eaten raw, though a small amount of salt or soy on them enhances their flavor.

Insects should be rinsed before consumption. For more mobile insects, such as grasshoppers and ants, place them in a tight-mesh pasta strainer and cover the open top with cheesecloth, then run water over them. Once clean, the insects should be placed in a plastic bag, sealed, and set in the freezer for approximately one-quarter to one-half hour. The freezer will act as a relatively humane way of terminating their life function . . . ah hell, they're bugs. You know they wouldn't give you any kind of consideration.

DOG

The dog has recently been reclassified as a member of the same species as the wolf, as opposed to being a unique species unto itself. Scientists have concluded that dogs were bred from wolves to be working animals (sheep dogs, for example), and to guard humans, property, and livestock. They were also bred as a food animal, much as cattle, sheep, goats, and pigs. While the thought of eating a family pet may be uncomfortable to westerners, the meat of dogs is reported to be quite flavorful.

Some Native American cultures used dog as a food source, as did the Celtic societies in Europe. The Maya ate dog, specially raised on a vegetarian diet that improved flavor. Spanish ships returning from Central and South America did sometimes carry salted dog meat for the trip, though the meat source was not widely accepted.

Dog is still consumed in parts of Asia, including Korea, where there have been attempts to reclassify the animal as livestock, thus legalizing its consumption and giving the government the right to regulate the restaurants that serve the meat. The particular breed of dog most often eaten is called *nurungi* in Korean (also known as "yellow dog").

The main reasons for eating dog meat are simple and practical. Dogs are easily raised and are not picky about what they are fed, and produce a reasonable amount of meat. In terms of sociological views or taboos about eating what is a pet in the eyes of most westerners, other cultures do not necessarily view them the same way and may have similar views about the consumption of beef, veal, or other livestock.

For those protective of puppies but not so fond of cats, the eating of cats is not unknown, but they produce significantly lower yields of meat, and they are greasy and have a less palatable flavor.

Alien Stuff

HOW TO MAKE CROP CIRCLES

Making a crop circle takes some planning and preparation, but the time and tools required are not significant.

1. Tools: One-hundred-foot surveyor's tape, a stalk-stomper (a six-foot board with a rope attached to each end, forming a large loop), sod roller, hooded flashlights. A dowsing rod is optional, if you choose to align the circle with local Earth energies, but not required.

2. Plan: Location is important. Choose a location based upon visibility. A small hill improves the odds that the local or national press will get good photos. Also, maximum credibility occurs when the new circle is near the site of other circles.

   Design the circle ahead of time, to scale. Bring the plan, but be familiar with it and be judicious in the use of flashlights to avoid tipping off locals.

3. Execution: English crop circle artists recommend hanging out at the local pub until after dark. A tavern may be substituted in North America. Do not leave the pub until after dark, and make sure you are not followed. Unload the tools near the site, then stash the car someplace safe and hidden.

   When moving through the crops, be sure to follow the tractor lines to avoid damage to the crops—a good crop circle doesn't destroy the grain, just repositions it. Check local laws to be sure you are not risking serious criminal prosecution if apprehended.

   Set the center point of your circle. Stand on one foot while turning in a full circle, dragging the other foot over the crops to flatten them.

   Have your partner stand in the center of the circle, holding one end of the tape. Walk out from there holding the other end until the maximum radius is reached, then walk in a circle using the tape. Be sure to walk in the same direction as you spun for your center circle—this gives a more consistent, believable result.

Begin rolling or stomping. The direction you choose creates interesting patterns. Rolling out straight out from the center creates a radial pattern. A spiral in or out gives a feel of concentric circles.

With practice, the crop circle artist can create patterns in the flattened stalks, or leave standing areas. Added touches include smaller circles outside the main circle (called "grapeshot" by experts) or subsidiary circles, spirals, and connections to other circles.

4. "Authenticity": Crop circle artists say the community of believers in circles (those who think they represent the work of aliens or supernatural forces) will accept your circle as genuine if:

- The pattern has a link to some significant physical feature (an abandoned ancient city, for example), myth, or other aspect of the supernatural or UFO world (such as excerpts of text from the lost city of Atlantis, other circles, etc.).
- The field was being watched by believers while you were making the circle (and they didn't catch you).
- Strange lights, atmospherics, or sounds occur the night of the creation.
- You are not caught. (If no one sees you doing it, it's aliens. If they catch you and some beered-up buddies, it's trespassing.)

The Weird and the Morbid

HOW TO MAKE YOUR OWN SKELETON

Up until 1987, human skeletons were largely supplied to the world from India. Now the majority of bones come from China. A complete skeleton can be purchased, as can a specific bone group or individual bones, but the cost may range from a few hundred to a few thousand dollars.

- Jim Fixx, one of the "fathers" of jogging, died of a heart attack in 1984 while he was jogging.
- Attila the Hun died in A.D. 453 from a nosebleed on his wedding night.

The cleaning of a skeleton, that is removing the extraneous soft tissues and material from it, can be done at home, though it must be done with care to avoid damaging the bones.

Bones should never be boiled or bleached. The heat from boiling causes residual fats to soak into the bones, making them greasy and yellow. The fat and grease can be removed with ammonia or solvents, but this is not a pleasant task and will not remove fat that has soaked in deep.

Bleaching the bones will do permanent damage to the bones' structure, and over time it will cause them to crack or break down.

To properly clean a skeleton, there are two good methods. First is to use natural bacteria. All excess tissue that can be removed should be done with a sharp knife, exercising caution to avoid damage to the bones or injury to yourself. Kevlar or heavy leather gloves should be worn throughout the initial cleaning. The bones are then immersed in a container of clean water. The container is placed in a warm but well-ventilated location. The smell will be unpleasant.

The water should be poured out periodically (it makes good fertilizer for the garden), and replaced with a fresh batch. This is repeated as necessary until the water runs clear. At that point, the bones are clean. As a final step, the bones are soaked in off-the-shelf hydrogen peroxide. The longer they are in the peroxide, the whiter they will become. The peroxide will also act as a sterilizer.

The second method is to use dermestid beetles, which are small meat-eating insects commonly used in museums for this task. It isn't the beetles, though, so much as the larvae that do the job. They are particularly good for delicate jobs. The beetles can be purchased at biological supply houses, and a modest number is enough to start. They will reproduce and expand into a colony quickly enough.

The beetles should be set up in an enclosed container, preferably where they cannot get out, in a warm place. If they get out, they may eat things that they should not.

The bones should be placed in the container and checked periodically. A smallish bone will take a day or two to clean. The larger the specimen, the longer it will take. The larvae will not eat hide, hair, or feathers, but otherwise they are not particular about what they consume.

- The ashes of the average cremated person weigh nine pounds.
- The average human body contains enough
  - iron to make a three-inch nail;
  - sulfur to kill all fleas on an average dog;
  - carbon to make nine hundred pencils;
  - potassium to fire a toy cannon;
  - fat to make seven bars of soap;
  - phosphorus to make 2,200 match heads;
  - water to fill a ten-gallon tank.
- The average human produces 25,000 quarts of spit in a lifetime, enough to fill two swimming pools.

WHERE ARE THEY NOW (BESIDES DEAD)?

Final Resting Places of Famous People

Elvis Aron Presley: Graceland Estate, Memphis, Tennessee

Jimi Hendrix: Greenwood Memorial Park, Renton, Washington

Bruce and Brandon Lee: Lakeview Cemetery, Lot 276, Seattle, Washington

President George Washington: Mount Vernon Estate, Mount Vernon, Virginia

Marilyn Monroe (Norma Jean Baker): Westwood Memorial Park, Corridor of Memories, Crypt 24, Los Angeles, California

Paul "Bear" Bryant: Elmwood Cemetery, Birmingham, Alabama

Ty Cobb: Royston Cemetery, Royston, Georgia

Mel Blanc: Hollywood Forever Cemetery, Section 13, Pineland Section, Lot 149, right by the road, Hollywood, California

Chris Farley: Resurrection Cemetery, Madison, Wisconsin

John Belushi: Abel Hill Cemetery, Chilmark, Massachusetts

Toto (real name, Terry): Carl Spitz's backyard, Hollywood, California

George Herman "Babe" Ruth: Gate of Heaven Cemetery, Section 25, plot 1115, in the center of graves 3 and 4, Hawthorne, New York

Lee Marvin: Arlington National Cemetery, Arlington, Virginia

William "Billy the Kid" Bonney: Old Fort Sumner Cemetery, Fort Sumner, New Mexico

George Armstrong Custer: West Point U.S. Military Academy Post Cemetery, Section 27, Row A, Grave 1, West Point, New York

Erwin Rommel: Herrlingen Cemetery, Herrlingen, Germany

FAMOUS MORBID FIRSTS AND LASTS

Someone Had to Be the First or the Last

- Bridget Bishop was the first of the "witches" to be executed in Salem, Massachusetts, in 1692. Of the thirty-one "witches" tried, all were condemned to death, mostly by hanging. None of them were burned.
- Drawing and quartering ended in England in 1803. The last person executed in this manner was Edward Despard.
- Gary Gilmore was the first person executed after the restoration of the death penalty in the United States, by firing squad, in 1977. People drew lots for a chance at plugging Gary.
- The first fatality in a plane was Thomas A. Selfridge in 1908. He was a passenger when Wilbur Wright crashed a plane being tested for the U.S. War Department.
- The first person to die in space was Vladimir Komarov, a Russian cosmonaut. He was killed in 1967 on *Soyuz* 1.
- Mark Maples was the first person to be killed at Disneyland. He was thrown from the Matterhorn Bobsled in 1964 when he stood up.

THE MILITARY AND THINGS THAT GO BOOM

If the ability to use an opposable thumb is what separates man from beast, then the likelihood of blowing off said thumb is what separates man from woman.

Ka-BOOM

EXPLOSIVES

Explosions come in three basic types: mechanical, chemical, and nuclear.

Mechanical explosions are events like the rupture of an overfilled air tank or a steam explosion in a hot water heater. Mechanical explosions are dangerous but don't typically pack a significant punch, not on par with chemical explosions or nuclear detonations. Still, don't stand in front of a hot water tank when it goes.

The most familiar explosives are chemical. A chemical explosion happens when a material breaks down, either by burning or chemical decomposition, releasing a large amount of heat and energy very quickly in the process. The rapid reaction causes a fast expansion outward of hot gas, producing a shock wave.

Chemical explosives are classified as either combustion type or detonation type. Gunpowder is a combusting explosive—it burns very fast. A detonation-type explosive is set off by a sudden shock to the material. Nitroglycerin is a detonation-type explosive. Detonating explosives can be further broken down to primary and secondary types. A primary explosive is set off by a source such as a flame, spark, or impact, as long as it produces sufficient heat. Secondary types require a detonator and, in a few cases, a booster.

Gunpowder, smokeless powder, and black powder all combust or burn. Pour them out on the ground and set a match to them and they'll burn fast—but that's all. To make them explode, they must be confined and contained long enough for the gas they rapidly produce to build up pressure. This is how guns work— igniting the explosive in the end of a cartridge causes pressure to build rapidly (while being held back for a fraction of a second by the bullet) until sufficient pressure is reached to make the bullet leave the barrel very fast.

Following this to a logical end, it is generally true that any flammable substance can become an explosive if you can make it burn very fast and contain the pressure long enough. Lots of vapors and dusts can be quite explosive when they are mixed with oxygen and contained properly. Vaporized gasoline and oxygen in an engine cylinder are a form of controlled explosive.

Some dusts, such as those produced by coal mining, flour mills,

- **Dynamite can be set on fire without exploding. A detonator is required to make it go off.**
- **Modern explosive propellants have a variable burning speed. Otherwise they would burn so fast the barrel of the gun or cannon would split.**
- **The recipe for black powder is 75 percent saltpeter, 15 percent charcoal, and 10 percent sulfur. Animal dung is a great source of nitrates, which is why many bird-infested South Pacific islands were mined out for their deposits of guano. Remember, even black powder is dangerous. Be careful.**

wood mills, and sugar plants, can be very explosive. Under the right circumstances, a spark can cause a fire in the dust cloud that travels so quickly that it acts as a type of explosive.

Most burning-type explosives require oxygen to be available to support combustion. Some take advantage of the oxygen in the surrounding air, but this is not terribly effective. Others carry their own with them. The saltpeter (potassium nitrate) in black powder, for example, provides the oxygen the explosive needs to burn properly.

There are a few explosives, such as nitrogen iodide, that require no oxygen. When detonated, the compound splits, creating heat and causing the expansion of the material.

Nukes are a whole separate class unto themselves. See "The Big Boys—Nuclear Weapons" on page 121 for more information.

BLACK POWDER—A LITTLE HISTORY

No one can positively identify the inventor of the first known explosive, but at some point in time someone mixed saltpeter (potassium nitrate), sulfur, and charcoal in just the right proportions and put a match to it—probably unintentionally. The result must have been impressive enough to warrant continued study, refinement, and use.

The Chinese traditionally get the credit for doing this in the tenth century. They did not immediately see or choose to use black powder in military applications. They used it mostly for entertainment and signaling. At first. There is a written record that by the thirteenth century, they were using it to fire rocks out of reinforced bamboo tubes (an early form of mortar).

There is evidence that the Arabs may have invented black powder independently, and they certainly deserve credit for inventing the first gun (also in the thirteenth century), a bamboo tube reinforced with iron that shot an arrow. It is also possible that, given the trade between China and the Arab world, the idea may have started in one place and traveled to the other.

As a third possibility, an Englishman named Roger Bacon documented the recipe for black powder in 1242. He may have invented it, but he read Arabic and it is just as likely that he got the recipe from his readings or sources in the Middle East.

The Europeans were quick to find ways to use black powder to do damage. By the fourteenth century primitive muskets were in use in European nations, and after the late sixteenth and early seventeenth centuries most wars were fought with firearms as the predominant weapons over spears, swords, or other edged instruments.

The Europeans also began applying black powder to commercial and civil ventures, using it for mining and tunneling in the 1600s. It was first used in tunneling on the Malpas Tunnel in France in 1679.

MAKING BLACK POWDER

Black powder is produced by combining charcoal and sulfur with steel balls in a metal drum. The drum is rotated, causing the balls to crush and mix the charcoal and sulfur. This is called a "ball mill." Saltpeter is processed separately with steel rollers. The three materials are mixed and heated while being turned and stirred, then ground and mixed further with water added to keep the mix damp.

After this, the powder is fed through wooden rollers to break up lumps, and then pressed into cakes. The cakes are broken up into manageable slabs, and then run through a corning mill, which breaks them up into grains. The grains are glazed, tumbled in wooden cylinders until they are rounded, and dried by blowing air through them. Adding powdered graphite during this process puts a thin coating (the glazing) on the grains, provides some protection against water, and causes the powder to flow smoothly.

Black powder has been replaced almost entirely with modern smokeless powders and high explosives such as nitroglycerin, dynamite, mercury fulminate, and gun cotton.

DYN-O-MITE!

Nitroglycerin was discovered by an Italian chemist, Ascanio Sobrero, in 1847. It is highly unstable and does not react well to sudden shocks or impacts. As a result, it was difficult to use it safely in military or commercial applications. Alfred Nobel developed dynamite as a safer alternative to nitroglycerin in 1875. One of the casualties of his experiments was his brother.

Dynamite is a mixture of nitroglycerin and an absorbent filler (often known as "dope") such as wood pulp, sawdust, or other material. When Nobel first developed dynamite, he used *kieselguhr*, a type of diatomaceous soil, as his dope. (Diatoms are tiny plants, and diatomaceous soils contain their fossils. This type of material is also used to create the mild abrasive found in toothpaste.)

BETTER LIVING THROUGH PLASTIC EXPLOSIVES

Plastic explosives are both a highly useful part of the military inventories of the world, and a very useful material for peaceful civilian uses. They're light, stable, and easy to form into custom shapes and needs. They pack a very considerable punch.

The two most popular types are the Czech-produced Semtex and its American counterpart, Composition 4 (more commonly known as C4). Both feel like a semisoft plastic, similar in texture to Play-Doh.

Both are very difficult to spot on a simple X-ray machine. They have no smell that a human can detect, and can only be spotted with sophisticated chemical sniffers, explosives detection systems (EDS) now used in American airports to scan baggage, or trained dogs.

Semtex is composed of two other explosives, cyclonite (also known as RDX) and pentaerythrite tetranitrate (known as PETN). Both are stable and difficult to set off accidentally. Normally, a blasting cap or detonator cord is needed. Semtex is the explosive responsible for the bringing down Pan Am 103 over Lockerbie, Scotland—it is estimated that only six ounces were required—and a French DC-10 over Chad.

The United States uses C4 in military applications. In particular, it comes as the M118 composition C4 Block demolition charge. In this configuration it is a sheet explosive, packed by the half-pound with pressure-sensitive adhesive tape on the back. It can be cut into different shapes and stuck to almost any surface, then detonated with an M8 blasting cap. It is highly effective as a cutting charge or breaching charge, and is not affected by water (though the tape doesn't stick to wet, dirty, rusty, or frozen surfaces).

C4 should never be ingested, as it is poisonous, even though its consistency is not too far off from chewing gum.

M-80S AND CHERRY BOMBS

M-80s were designed for military use as a gunfire simulator. Each one is an inch and a half long, nine-sixteenths of an inch in diameter, and contains forty-five grains of explosives. A grain is equal to 64.8 milligrams. An M-80 has enough power to remove a hand or disintegrate a USPS-approved mailbox—which is not something that should be done under any circumstances as it is a federal crime.

Cherry bombs are round, usually three-quarters of an inch in diameter. Their outer shell is composed of sawdust bound up with sodium silicate, and dyed red. They're not as powerful as M-80s, but are capable of causing significant harm.

M-80s and cherry bombs are no longer available to the public because the U.S. Congress passed a law called the Child Protection Act in 1966. It made M-80s—and cherry bombs in particular—illegal, including owning, selling, or using them *anywhere* in the jurisdiction of the United States.

The law goes further, limiting firecrackers in the United States to contain not more than 50 milligrams of "pyrotechnic compound." An M-80 contains about fifty times that amount.

Many fireworks stands sell lines of fireworks and firecrackers that are marketed under the M-80 or Cherry Bomb brands, and M-80 substitutes that go by names such as the "M-70," "M-50," and others. These should not be confused with the real items. They are lightweights.

- Nitro was used as a headache remedy under the name "Glonoin."
- The Molotov cocktail is any makeshift bomb using gasoline or other flammable substance poured into a breakable container (a bottle or jar) with a rag or cloth wick in the mouth. The wick is lit and the whole contraption is thrown at the intended target. As the glass breaks, the burning wick ignites the liquid and sets fire to the target.

The Molotov cocktail was named for the Soviet Vyacheslav Mikhailovich Molotov, the head of the Council of People's Commissars (1930–1941) and foreign minister (1939–1949 and 1953–1956). In 1956 when Hungarian partisans used them against the Russians, the Hungarians named them the "Molotov cocktail" in honor of the Soviet foreign minister.

HOW DOES A FIREWORK WORK?

Generally speaking, if black powder is packed in a tube with a fuse attached, it will make a bang, especially if the tube is hardy enough to let the explosive pressure of the burning powder build up a bit.

If an opening is left at one end of the tube, the gas will exit that way, making a primitive skyrocket. Proper skyrockets require fins and a launching stake of some kind.

Aerial shells are more akin to military mortars than skyrockets, combining a launching charge with a display charge. Fine black powder is mixed with various chemicals, which determine how they look when ignited, and formed into pellets or "stars." For example, adding charcoal to the outer shell of black powder will produce a flaming tail as the shell rises. Sodium in the stars makes a red color, copper makes green, barium blue, and aluminum or magnesium white.

The stars are packed loosely inside a shell (of paper or thin clay), with coarse black powder packed around it. A fuse is attached to the shell. When the fuse is lit, the outer layer of black powder burns and launches the shell up the mortar tube. As the outer shell burns through to the inner shell, the fine gunpowder explodes and expels the stars, also causing them to ignite. How the shells are packed and made determines the spread and burn pattern and thus the way they look from the ground.

Most fireworks sold in the United States are made in Japan, China, Taiwan, or Korea.

THE BIG BOYS—NUCLEAR WEAPONS

Nuclear weapons operate by either splitting apart or fusing together atoms. The energy released when this is done suddenly and with a particular mass of radioactive material causes an explosion, anywhere up to the equivalent of several million tons of TNT.

Uranium and plutonium are two of the most common materials used in making nuclear weapons. Uranium is a naturally occurring element, though its most common form, U-238, is not good for nuclear weapons. (The 238 refers to the isotope of the atom, a measure of the number of protons and neutrons in the nucleus. Uranium always has 92 protons, but the number of neutrons can vary. In U-238, there are 146 neutrons—146 plus 92 protons equals 238.) Another isotope of uranium, U-235, is much better for nuclear weapons, but is rare in nature. Weapons makers create it in a variety of ways, "enriching" natural uranium to make a better bomb. Plutonium is not a natural element, but is made by enriching uranium in a nuclear reactor.

Over time, uranium or plutonium decay, spitting out neutrons and reducing themselves slowly to other elements. Over time, for example, uranium becomes lead. If the process of spitting out the neutrons is accelerated, the released neutrons will strike other uranium or plutonium atoms, causing them to split and spit out more neutrons, which in turn strike other atoms. This causes a chain reaction. Under controlled conditions, such as in the core of a nuclear reactor, heat is produced and energy created.

If the chain reaction is speeded up by violently compressing a given mass of U-235 or plutonium in on itself, there is an explosion. Large amounts of heat are released, as is gamma radiation (very bad stuff). The normal method of accomplishing this is to separate two carefully machined pieces of U-235, then drive them together very suddenly and accurately using chemical explosives. One of the most difficult challenges of the Manhattan Project (aside from making the quantity of U-235 needed) was to develop the refined explosives and the precise firing circuits required to initiate the chain reaction.

Some nuclear weapons use fusion, which is the forcing together of atomic nuclei, usually hydrogen isotopes, to form helium. This is the same mechanism the sun uses, fusing the lightest element into the next heavier one on the periodic table. A fusion reaction requires a great deal of energy to initiate, and for weapons the firing mechanism is typically a fission device (using uranium or plutonium). Fusion reactions are not terribly radioactive, but the fission reaction required to start them is.

- Uranium is naturally radioactive, as is plutonium. Uranium, though, can be handled relatively safely. The primary risk is assembling a supercritical mass of it (enough that it decides to go into a chain reaction by itself). This is unlikely, and besides, even a supercritical mass will not explode unless it is forced together suddenly and with great pressure. Plutonium is also highly unlikely to go critical arbitrarily, but it's very poisonous. A microscopic particle of it inhaled or ingested will kill you.
- The first nuclear detonation was at the Alamagordo Bombing Range in New Mexico, in a desert called Jornada del Muerto (Journey of Death).
- The first nuclear device detonated was called the "gadget," and the test was code-named Trinity.
- The major atomic test sites are Nevada, Eniwetok Atoll, Johnson Island (United States), Christmas Island and Australia (United Kingdom), French Polynesia and North Africa (France), and Novaya Zemlya and Semipalatinsk (former U.S.S.R.).
- Did you know? Phosgene, a deadly gas used in chemical warfare, smells like new-mown hay.

The largest nuclear bombs known were able to exceed 20 mega-tons. The smallest are reported to be suitcase-sized, with a yield as small as 0.5 kilotons.

At the present time, the following nations have overt nuclear weapons capability:

> Britain
> China
> France
> India
> Pakistan
> Russia
> United States

Israel is suspected to have nuclear weapons, but they aren't talking. Evidence strongly suggests that Iran, Iraq, Libya, North Korea, and South Africa have them or have tried to build them. North Korea claimed to have ceased attempts in 1994, and the South African government is reported to have built six uranium-fueled bombs which have since been dismantled. Three members of the former Soviet Union (Belarus, Kazakhstan, and the Ukraine) had nuclear weapons, but returned them to the Russians.

UH-OH . . .

In the Cold War lingo of the Pentagon, a "nucflash" was the accidental or unauthorized detonation of a nuclear weapon that might lead to an exchange of weapons between the United States and the former U.S.S.R.—this never happened. A "broken arrow" was an accident that involved nuclear weapons without the risk of a war starting between the U.S. and the former U.S.S.R., but including nonnuclear explosions of weapons (the high explosives), radioactive contamination, and the loss of a nuclear weapon or part of a nuclear weapon. A few examples:

- In 1950 a B-36 bomber dropped a nuclear weapon off the coast of British Columbia. The bomb's high explosive did detonate on impact, but the bomb did not go off. The plane crashed, but the crew parachuted to safety.
- In 1956 a B-47 bomber at Lakenheath Royal Air Force Base in England crashed into a bomb storage facility containing at least three nuclear weapons.
- In 1957 a bomber accidentally dropped a ten-megaton bomb near Albuquerque, New Mexico. To the relief of all concerned, it did not detonate.
- A B-47 crashed at a U.S. air base in Morocco in 1958. The bomber was loaded with nuclear weapons and burned for several hours before the fire was controlled. Fortunately the bombs did not detonate, though the area was contaminated.
- In 1966 a B-52 collided with an aerial tanker over Palomares, Spain, causing the planes to crash. Four hydrogen bombs were released. Two ruptured, scattering radioactive waste over Palomares, one landed at a farm, and the fourth was recovered after deep-water searches turned it up.
- In 1980 routine maintenance on a Titan II missile in its silo caused a fuel leak and explosion, launching the missile and reentry vehicle from the silo. The warhead was recovered.

You're in the Army Now . . .

BODY ARMOR

Humans began protecting themselves with purpose-designed leather, cloth, and metal armor at least three-thousand years ago, and by the time of the Middle Ages in Europe and Japan, the making of armor had become a specialty science, incorporating refined metals worked into plates and intricately assembled coats of chain mail.

Body armor as it is known today is soft and flexible, more like a heavy vest or coat than the suits of steel worn by knights and soldiers in the past. The first practical modern attempts at armor of this type began shortly after the assassination of President William McKinley in 1901. Law enforcement officers and others began experimenting with protective vests made from reinforced silk. The early results were effective against low-velocity (traveling at less than four hundred feet per second) handgun bullets, but improvements in ammunition and increases in bullet velocity made the vests less effective.

Ballistic nylon "flak jackets" were introduced during World War II, but were primarily designed to stop shell fragments and were ineffective against rifles, pistols, and other ballistic ammunition. Heavier armor was also worn, often incorporating steel plating, but proved impractical if the wearer needed to move quickly and easily. Lighter-weight versions of this type of armor were used in Vietnam, but the weight and discomfort

- Contrary to popular images and movies, the Vikings did not wear horns on their helmets. For practical reasons, a functional helmet is designed to shed blows from weapons, and excess ornamentation—such as horns—would have been counter to this goal.
- Archduke Ferdinand of Austria was reportedly wearing a silk protective vest when he was shot and killed in Serbia (which precipitated the First World War). The assassin shot the Archduke in the head.

of wearing them in a hot, humid environment made them less than practical.

Modern body armor is made of tightly woven and very strong fibers (such as Kevlar), strong enough to stop the impact of bullets (short of high-powered rifles). The fabric slows the round long enough for it to spread and dissipate its force without penetrating the vest. The impact is still substantial and causes "blunt trauma," similar to being hit very hard with a hard object. Heavier grades of body armor incorporate metal or ceramic panels that will stop high-powered weapons. Tactical vests often combine the two, using small plates on the chest and spine to give a higher degree of protection to critical spots without burdening the wearer with the weight of a heavier vest.

THE MODERN HELMET

Soldiers in the armies of the nineteenth century had abandoned metal helmets as they were useless against cannon fire and the muskets of the era. Only a few soldiers continued to wear metal helmets, and then largely for show. The reintroduction of the metal helmet as an everyday part of modern military combat gear dates from 1915, when General August Louis Adrian of the French Army developed a steel cap that was worn under the cloth kepi used by the French Army. It was intended to provide protection against shell fragments. By the end of the First World War, helmets became ubiquitous in almost every army.

When the U.S. Army entered the First World War, it was unprepared in terms of equipment and material. The American Expeditionary Force (AEF) adopted weapons, equipment, and even some uniforms from their French and British allies. The "doughboy" helmet with its rounded top and wide, flared brim came from the British, and was the standard of the U.S. military until the beginning of the Second World War.

Early on in that war, the U.S. Army introduced the M1 helmet, which provided better protection than the old British model by covering the ears and more of the head. It had a manganese steel shell and liner, and weighed over two pounds. Over twenty-two million of them were produced during the war alone, and they were used in Korea and Vietnam.

In the 1980s, the U.S. military adopted the PASGT Kevlar helmets. The new U.S. helmets are made of a Kevlar composite material, are lightweight, fire-resistant up to 375°F, and provide excellent protection against bullets, shrapnel, and shell fragments. Further, a polyurethane coating allows easy decontamination after exposure to chemical agents.

INTELLIGENCE TIDBIT

During World War II, the German military used a coding machine called the Enigma, which used a very complex form of substitution (changing one letter for another) to encrypt messages. The machines used rotating disks to change the substitution code after each message was typed in by the code operator, so that a different code was used for each message typed. The Germans also changed the code setup every day to confuse the enemy's attempts at decoding. The resistance of Enigma-coded messages to deciphering was estimated to be so high that a code analyst, trying a different combination every minute, twenty-four hours a day, would require more time than the age of the universe to check all possible scenarios.

As it happens, the Polish government began working on methods and decoding machines (called *bombes*) to decode the messages. Part of their early success was based upon acquiring the wiring diagrams for the Enigmas from an unhappy German civil servant prior to start of the Second World War. Just before the invasion of Poland by the

German Army in 1939, the Poles turned over the plans for the Enigmas and the *bombes* to the British, along with all the information the Polish intelligence services had developed for decoding the German messages.

The British succeeded in cracking the codes, even when the Germans made changes that increased the complexity of the coding to the point of being completely unbreakable—statistically.

In large part, this was due to the analysis and work of a British mathematician, Alan Turing (who also described the basic concept for the "Turing machine," the forerunner of the modern programmable computer), and some basic logical reductions of the way the Enigmas worked and the way the German intelligence services coded and formatted messages. The British used other tips, such as the fact that many messages started with the same small group of words repeated twice, giving the code breakers a hint to the starting point of the codes and the Enigma setup for that day. As a result, for most of the Second World War, the Allies were able to read German secure information.

• The only living relative of Adolph Hitler was his nephew, Patrick Hitler. He served in the United States Navy during the Second World War, but saw no combat.

A little-known fact is that after the war, the British captured many thousands of the Enigma machines, a large number of which were given to the governments of their colonies and former colonies to use for their own purposes, such as sending secret information from embassies to their capitols. It appears that the British, who did not acknowledge their success in cracking Enigma until the 1970s, were able to read the mail of their former colonies for almost thirty years as a result.

NAVY SEALS

SEAL. Short for "sea, air, land," the SEALs trace their roots to the Navy frogmen of World War II. They were formally created on January 1, 1962, by President John F. Kennedy. They have become popular in Hollywood (the various films of Steven Segal, Demi Moore's *G.I. Jane,* and Charlie Sheen's *Navy SEALs*) and the former governor of Minnesota, the Honorable Jesse Ventura, was a SEAL, raising their visibility in the public eye.

> • Each of the SEALs' sixteen-man platoon is allocated 1.5 million rounds of ammunition each year for target practice and training.

SEALs go through twenty-seven weeks of very intense and specialized training, a program designed to teach them their craft and to toughen them in the extreme. The course includes seven weeks of rigorous physical training and swimming in preparation for the program. The second phase of the training includes classroom and practical training. The last training phase focuses on underwater-demolitions training and above-water skills. The entire program teaches the SEALs to be self-reliant and to endure hardship and extreme discomfort, but also to work in a team.

Assuming a recruit doesn't wash out or quit of his own accord, after completing the course he will be on probation for six months.

SEALs train constantly, honing their crafts, none more so than marksmanship. The teams must practice close-quarter fighting constantly, shooting three hundred or more rounds of ammunition per week. Considering the specifications of their weapons, this means they will wear out their Berreta 92F 9mm pistols every twelve months. Their primary weapon, the MP-5 machine gun, will last only slightly longer at this rate of fire.

DELTA FORCE

The United States Army operates its own elite strike unit, commonly known as the Delta Force. More properly called First SFOD-Delta, it was formed in 1977 as a counterterrorism force in response to the world political climate. Delta was modeled on Britain's Special Air Services (SAS), and consists of three assault teams or squadrons (designated A, B, and C).

Delta Force training is reported to be on par with that of the Navy SEALs, with a few differences. Both forces pride themselves on being able to go anywhere anytime courtesy of the Air Force Special Operations Command or the Army's 160th Special Aviation Regiment, but Delta doesn't work in the water the way the SEALs do—though both forces work together. In particular, Delta teams pride themselves on their marksmanship and close-quarter battle (CQB) skills, such as storming buildings or airplanes, eliminating all terrorists, and protecting the lives of hostages.

Membership in Delta Force is by invitation only, and candidates are typically selected from the Green Berets or Army Rangers. They must go through an eighteen-day selection process prior to training. Assuming they make it through this, each selectee starts a six-month training cycle with emphasis on shooting, air assaults, protection, high-speed driving, and covert operations. Typical Deltas are in their early thirties and have above-average intelligence and physical capabilities.

The exact size and composition of Delta is not public, but is estimated at eight thousand, including men and women. The Deltas are at home at Fort Bragg on Range 19.

SPAM

It's chopped and pressed. It comes in a squared-off can for ease of stacking. It's really good to eat fried (especially when you're in the woods). What more can we say? It's SPAM.

SPAM

SPAM, the amazing meat food product in a can. It has been the brunt of jokes, songs (remember the Vikings singing "SPAM, SPAM, SPAM" in *Monty Python's Flying Circus*?), and comedy acts for years. In terms of notoriety, it's probably got even the infamous Twinkie beat.

SPAM was first produced by Hormel in 1937 under the name of Spiced Ham. Contracting and combining the two words resulted in the word "SPAM" (note, always in capital letters). According to Hormel, they have produced over five billion cans and branched out into specialty areas, including low-fat, low-sodium, smoke-flavored, and oven-roasted turkey, and of course the original (made from pork shoulder, ham, and secret spices).

SPAM basics:

- The distinctive rectangular can was introduced in the 1940s as a way of saving space in shipping.
- Hawaiians eat more SPAM than anyone else. You'll find SPAM fried with rice, used as an accompaniment to saimen (a noodle dish), scrambled with eggs, and served in loco moco (white rice, fried egg, and brown gravy).
- Overseas, SPAM sells best in the United Kingdom and South Korea (you can get it in a gift box in Korea).
- You must drive thirty-five miles on a snowmobile in−30°F weather to fully brown a can of SPAN on the engine.
- SPAM-carving contests have become regular events in the United States.

Visit the SPAM museum, located in a mall in Austin, Minnesota, where you can see SPAM through the years, or attend SPAM-Jam in Austin to partake of some good eating and good fun.

SPAMMING

SPAM and the Internet. If you've got email, you will get "unsolicited commercial email," known as UCE or "spam." In many cases, spam is sent out to a broad-sweep of email accounts, generally plugging up these locations and putting unnecessary traffic on the Internet. How this kind of traffic became known as spam is not clear, but Hormel has a very specific opinion about it. This is a direct quote from the official SPAM website:

> We oppose the act of "spamming" or sending unsolicited commercial email (UCE). We have never engaged in this practice, although we have been victimized by it. If you have been one of those who has received UCE with a return address using our website address of SPAM.com, it wasn't us. It's easy and commonplace for somebody sending UCE to simply adopt a fake header ID, which disguises the true source of the UCE and makes it appear that it is coming from someone else. If you have or do receive UCE with this header ID, please understand that it didn't come from us.

The makers of SPAM are clear that while they do not object to the use of the term "spam," they do object to the use of their product image with the term. They observed the attempt by Lucasfilm to prevent the use of the term "Star Wars" in relationship to the Strategic Defense Initiative. The Federal District Court ruled that there is no infringement or harm done, so that people may use trade names in describing people or things (a "Teflon" politician, "Mickey Mouse" behavior, and "Cadillac" solutions) without fear of legal action.

GRUB AND A STOGIE

Being a guy means taking care of yourself. Get some exercise (we don't cover that), plenty of rest (we're sure you can figure that one out on your own), eat the right foods (chili and ketchup have never been properly recognized by the Food and Drug Administration), and if you do smoke, don't smoke crap.

Hot Food

REALLY HOT FOOD—THE CHILI PEPPER

When eating a chili pepper or food with chilies in it, a chemical in the chilies, capsaicin, irritates trigeminal cells in the mouth, nose, and stomach. These cells are sensory neurons. When exposed to the capsaicin they produce substance P, a neuropeptide messenger that sends a message of pain to the brain. After eating spicy foods regularly for an extended time, the repeated exposure damages the ability of the cells to function properly, which is why some people can develop a tolerance. The trade-off is decrease in the sense of taste.

The heat of a pepper is calculated in Scoville units, a measure developed in 1912. The way of determining the Scoville rating is to add sugar to a pepper solution until the taste of the pepper can no longer be identified (as such, it is a subjective method). The habanero pepper (see below) is reported to be the hottest, ranging from 100,000 to nearly 600,000 Scoville units, depending on the variety and the crop. A few other examples:

- A good bowl of chili will make you sweat below your eyes, but it won't overwhelm your taste buds. You should be able to finish it without stopping to cool off or rinse your mouth.
- William Gebhardt, a German immigrant in New Braunfels, Texas, created chili powder in 1902. It is still sold today under the Gebhardt brand.
- The first commercially produced taco sauce in the United States was introduces by La Victoria Foods in 1952.
- The first bottled cayenne pepper sauces were introduced in Massachusetts around 1807.
- McIlhenny's Tabasco Sauce was first commercially introduced in 1868. The manufacturer, Edmund McIlhenny, sent it out in recycled cologne bottles. The recipe for the sauce was patented in 1870.

- The chiltepin, rocoto, and Chinese *kwangs* range from 50,000 to 100,000
- The cayenne long, Tabasco, and Thai *prik khee nu* measure at 30,000 to 50,000
- Crushed red peppers are rated at 15,000 to 30,000
- Tabasco sauce and serrano peppers rate at 5,000 to 15,000
- Jalapeños are mild, averaging 2,500 to 5,000

Most peppers prefer high humidity and warm nights, and as such they are most common in Mexico and Central America, but they grow well in the southeastern United States and parts of California. Stressing the plants by underwatering them makes the peppers even hotter.

The habanero, reportedly the hottest pepper, comes in several varieties. Orange habaneros are the most common and are from the Yucatán area of Mexico. The red savina variety is the highest-rated in terms of heat, measuring in at 577,000 Scoville units.

Habenero peppers reside at the upper end of the Scoville scale and have an intense enough concentration of capsaicin that they can actually cause dermatitis (irritation of the skin), similar to poison ivy. The eyes are at particular risk. Wear gloves when handling and preparing hot peppers, and rinse the cutting surface with bleach and detergent afterward. Otherwise, the capsaicin will spread to other foods and surfaces. Capsaicin burns on the skin can be soothed with vegetable oil. If it gets into the eyes, an immediate flushing with water or eyewash is advised.

Indian scientists claim that the habanero is not the hottest pepper in the world. The *naga jolokia,* which is grown in the northeastern hills of the Assam region of India, has been rated by the Indians at 855,000 Scoville units. The rating has not been independently verified and for the moment the red savina variety of habanero is listed by the *Guinness Book of World Records* as the hottest.

ONCE THE BURNING BEGINS

There are a variety of theories and solutions to cooling a pepper burn in the mouth, including drinking water, milk, beer, or soda and eating sugar, bread, rice, or citrus fruits. The primary point is to wash away, dilute, or absorb the capsaicin (the chemical that causes the sensation of burning or heat).

Scientists tested solutions by having subjects chew a slice of serrano chili for one minute, and then trying various remedies. Results were based on how long the test subject took to report an alleviation of the pain. Water is the worst, taking up to eleven minutes to relieve the discomfort. Heavy fruit syrup or olive oil in water will take care of it in ten minutes. Milk is good, as is water and sugar, at seven minutes.

CHILI

The origin of chili cannot be determined exactly. One common story is that it started out as a kind of Texan pemmican. Early settlers to the territory pounded dried beef and beef fat, chile peppers, and salt to make a rot-resistant trail food. The mixture was boiled in pots along the trail, making an "instant" chili. The food may have been inspired by Native American cultures such as the Inca, Aztec, and Maya, all of whom were eating dishes using peppers and similar spices before Europeans arrived in the New World.

Chili comes in too many different forms and styles to be strictly classified, but the major categories are Texas-style and New Mexico–style. Texas-style chili is a meat chili and traditionally does not include beans. New Mexico–style chili is more similar to a vegetable stew with chili peppers, though it may include meat.

The essential ingredients—the things that make chili chili—are onions, peppers, and garlic. For meat chilis, shredded or cubed beef cooked long and slow so it is tender and flaky is optimal. Ground beef is acceptable, though purists denigrate it. A variety of different meats can be used, including pork, wild game, rattlesnake, and even chicken. Armadillo is not recommended due to its taste—it does not go well with the flavor of most peppers.

The chili broth may be red or green, depending on the chilies used. Proper chili does not use a tomato base, but if tomatoes are used, their flavor should always be subordinate to the taste of the chilies.

STUFF YOU CAN EAT IF YOU REALLY HAVE TO

BAALUT (Philippines): Fertilized duck or chicken egg, buried in the ground for a while to age.

HAKARL (Iceland): Fermented Greenland shark.

HAGGIS (Scotland): Sheep's stomach stuffed with oatmeal and spices and steamed.

VEGEMITE OR MARMITE (Australia): A sand- wich spread made from yeast, popular in Australia.

RICCI DE MARE (Italy): Raw sea urchin eggs.

HEADCHEESE: Like a cross between cheese and lunchmeat, headcheese is made from the heads of various animals.

LUTEFISK (Norway): A Norse delicacy, this is essentially dried cod treated with lye.

FROG'S LEGS (various countries): You know what they say . . . it tastes like chicken.

ESCARGOT (France): The ultimate form of garden control, instead of poisoning garden snails, you eat them with lots of garlic.

RETSINA (Greece): White wine with pine resin added.

BIRD'S NEST SOUP (China): Made using a material secreted by certain birds to bind their nests together.

- **Fugu,** the Japanese name for a delicacy made from pufferfish, can be a last meal. The fish produces a powerful chemical toxin called tetrodotoxin, which is over 250 times more potent than cyanide. Tetrodotoxin blocks signals between nerves and muscles, causing paralysis, convulsions, and death in about 60 percent of the poisonings each year. When sickness or death occurs, the fault lies with the chef who, while preparing the fish, failed to keep the meat from touching the internal organs, which contain the toxin.

- The term "corned beef" comes from the corn-kernel-sized chunks of salt that were packed around the beef to preserve it before soaking it in brine became the standard practice.

- The rainbow sheen you see on sliced beef, turkey, and ham is the result of a diffraction grating type effect that causes the light to split into its various colors. This is a result of the parallel bands of tissue and the liquid content of the meat.

- Canadian firms exported thirty-one metric tons of horsemeat to the United States in 1999. The meat was intended for animal feed.

THOUSAND-YEAR-OLD EGGS (China): Like baalut, this is a fermented egg.

KIM-CHEE (Korea): Spiced cabbage, fermented in a clay pot buried in a dung heap.

SEAL AND WHALE BLUBBER (various countries): Eat it hot and raw right from the animal carcass.

VELVEETA (North America): A processed food product, represented as a cheese of some type. Best eaten hot with bottled salsa mixed in and tortilla chips.

SAGO WORMS (Oceania): Beetle larva found in the heart of sago palms. Served roasted like a sausage.

WITCHETY GRUBS (Australia): Australian grubs, quite large, eaten raw or cooked.

MONKEY BRAINS (various): Eaten raw, fried, or mixed with other foods.

ROCKY MOUNTAIN OYSTERS (United States): Bull testicles, best served with onions and lightly sautéed in white wine.

HOW TO COOK AND PREPARE A RATTLESNAKE, TEXAS-STYLE

Fine one rattlesnake. These can be purchased, but fresh caught is best. For wild or free-run snake, they are best found in the early morning or evening. Approach the snake with caution, and pin it down at the neck with a stick. Caution should always be used when hunting rattlesnakes—their bite is venomous and can be fatal to humans.

After catching and subduing the snake, remove its head with an ax or machete. Remove the skin by pulling it down from the neck toward the tail in one steady pull. The flesh should be cleaned, including removing the entrails. Bones do not need to be removed but exercise caution when eating to avoid choking on them. Cut the meat into serving sizes, and then roll it in a batter of white flour, cracker crumbs, salt, pepper, and garlic, with water or beer added to make it sticky.

Fill a large metal pot with three inches of vegetable oil and heat until it will ignite a wooden match floating on the surface.

Fry the battered meat until golden brown. Remove with metal tongs and shake off the excess oil. Set each piece on a clean, dry paper towel for a few moments to soak up excess grease. Snake should always be served hot with Tabasco sauce or ketchup.

KETCHUP/CATSUP/CATCHUP

Ketchup most probably came from a Southeast Asian sauce similar to soy sauce, made from fish brine, herbs, and spices—but no tomatoes. European sailors returning from the Orient introduced the sauce to the West in the seventeenth century, and it was made with a variety of ingredients, including mushrooms, walnuts, and tomatoes. The only common element in all these sauces was the vinegar used in making them.

The word "catchup" first appeared in English in 1690, followed by "ketchup" in 1711, and "catsup" in 1730. The root of the word is probably from *kechap,* a Malaysian fish sauce. All three English spellings (ketchup, catchup, catsup) are correct.

- **Ketchup does not need to be made with tomatoes. A perfectly acceptable form can be made with bananas, blueberries, mushrooms, cranberries, or mangoes.**
- **Heinz was founded in 1869, but their first product was not ketchup. It was grated horseradish. Ketchup was not added to the company product line until 1876.**

Government regulations for ketchup include basic ingredients: tomato sauce, vinegar, sugar, salt, onion or garlic flavors, and spices. Grading standards for ketchup also dictate the rating based on the flow of the sauce. In 1953 grade A ketchup could not flow faster than nine centimeters in thirty seconds.

Standards have been revised. Ketchup is now called grade A if the flow is three to seven centimeters in thirty seconds.

LEA & PERRINS WORCESTERSHIRE SAUCE

In 1835, Lord Sandys, an English nobleman from Worcestershire, England, hired two chemists, John Lea and William Perrins, to try to duplicate a sauce he had come across during his travels in India. The sauce produced by Lea and Perrins was a disappointment to the Lord, and was abandoned to the cellar.

The sauce was left there, forgotten. One of chemists came across the brew two years later, and before discarding it, decided to give it a taste. Surprisingly, the sauce had fermented and matured, and the aroma and taste were quite good. Not too long thereafter, the sauce was introduced commercially and became a worldwide success. The sauce is made with tamarind, peppercorns, chili peppers, garlic, and anchovies, and is aged in wooden casks.

A Really Good Smoke

HANDMADE CIGARS

Good cigars take time and good raw materials to make. The best seeds are germinated for forty to forty-five days, then transplanted into rich soil. Once grown, the leaves are harvested, heaped up, and moistened to ferment. This process rids the leaves of excess ammonia. Fermented tobacco is baled in burlap and allowed to age anywhere from eighteen months to ten years.

A master blender creates the taste and style of the cigar by mixing together a combination of two to four different tobaccos. A cigar roller presses the leaves together in a mold to form the center of the cigar. This is called the "bunch." The bunch is then placed on a binder leaf and rolled to the right length and approximate shape.

(Many machine-made cigars use a homogenized bunch made of chopped tobacco—and sometimes other materials such as cellulose—which improves the uniformity of the burn, but makes for a less pleasant taste and makes the cigar dry out faster.)

- Sugar occurs in tobacco. The darker the natural color of the leaf, the more sugar and the sweeter the smoke.
- Book-style rolling means layering the filler leaves and then rolling them up like a scroll. Popular in Honduras. *Entubar*-style cigar making involves rolling each filler leaf back on itself, then binding the "tubes" together. This creates superior air flow and is popular in Cuba.
- Sigmund Freud, a cigar smoker himself, is credited with saying that a cigar was a phallic symbol. He neglected to mention that excessive enjoyment of phallic symbols is hazardous to your health. He died of cancer of the throat and mouth.
- Fidel Castro no longer smokes cigars. He gave them up in support of a public antismoking campaign.

The rough cigar is placed in a cigar mold and pressed for about an hour, rotated top to bottom once during the pressing. These are inspected and rolled in the wrapper (a half leaf of tobacco selected for both aesthetic appeal and flavor). A bit of glue is applied at the head of the wrapper leaf to hold it together, and then the cigars are inspected again for hard or soft spots, uniformity, and weight. Finished cigars are aged anywhere from 21 to 180 days.

PROPER CARE AND LIGHTING OF A GOOD CIGAR

Cigars should be kept in a humidor—a room or box with precisely controlled temperature and humidity—until they're to be smoked. The humidor will keep them from drying out, protecting the flavor. A humidor should be maintained at 70 percent humidity, at temperatures of 65 to 70°F. Cigars should never be stored in a refrigerator or freezer, which will dry the tobacco out and damage the flavor.

When smoking a cigar, the end should be clipped with a single- or double-bladed cutter, making a flat cut. Never use your teeth—it will leave a ragged opening and may snag the fibers in the leaf wrap, causing the cigar to unravel.

Use a cigar lighter, holding the fire below the tip of the cigar so the flame doesn't actually touch it. Matches should not be used unless they are sulfur-free. If using a candle, light a thin strip of cedar and use that to light the cigar.

Leave the band on the cigar until after you have clipped the head and had the first ten to twelve puffs. The band will help keep the cigar from unrolling after you clip the head.

CIGAR TERMS

Ring Gauge: The ring gauge refers to the diameter of the cigar measured in sixty-fourths of an inch. Thus, a ring gauge of 40 means the cigar is forty sixty-fourths of an inch around.

Parejos: The most common type of cigars. These are straight-sided cigars, and include Coronas, Panetelas, and Lonsdales.

Coronas: Midsized cigars, about seven inches long with a ring gauge of 47 or 48. Churchills are a type of Corona. A Gordo Corona (also called a Belicoso) is a shorter, fatter Corona, five or so inches long and up to 50 in ring gauge.

Panetelas: Generally longer and thinner than Coronas with a smaller ring gauge. Like the Corona, they also have an open foot and closed head. A Culebra is three Panetelas twisted together and banded.

Lonsdales: Thicker than the Panetela and slimmer and longer than a Corona, a Lonsdale will run to six and three-quarters inches with a 42 ring gauge.

CRIME, PUNISHMENT, AND THE POLICE

Face it, brother, there is something totally cool about the idea of cruising around in a black-and-white in your tactical body armor, a 12-gauge conveniently located on the dashboard (next to the cigarette lighter), looking for bad guys and perps. It is the ultimate in win-win situations—chicks dig it, you get to carry a gun, and best of all, you're doing it all in the name of the common good.

Stop in the Name of the Law

THE POLICE

American urban police forces were originally modeled on the London Metropolitan Police established in 1829 by Robert Peel (whose name is the source of two slang terms for police officers, "bobbies" and "peelers"). American police differ from those of other nations, though, in that most police forces are part of a national force, whereas Americans prefer a local authority to be responsible (with the obvious exception of state and federal law enforcement agencies). Another early distinction between American and foreign forces was that many of the systems of watchmen and constables required the person receiving the police service pay a fee, whereas American police were paid a salary by a government agency.

Permanent police forces grew from forces of watchmen or elected constables and were not common initially. New York's first regular force was created in 1845, though the force was composed of political appointees who patrolled in plain clothes. In 1853, when the city already had over 500,000 residents, the force was regularized with uniforms and permanent employment status rather than appointments. By the mid-1850s the officers commonly carried revolvers. Philadelphia followed in 1856, and Boston in 1859.

Black officers were not commonly accepted for general duty until the mid-1960s, though the city of New Orleans hired free blacks as early as 1814 to patrol predominantly black neighborhoods (as part of a city watchman program rather than a police force). The first full-time female patrol officers were introduced in Indianapolis in 1968.

The first regularized nonurban police force in the United States were the Texas Rangers. Founded in 1823 by Stephen F. Austin, the Rangers are now a special investigative branch of the Texas State Department of Public Safety. The Texas Rangers Hall of Fame is located on the banks of the Brazos River in Waco, Texas (also home of Dr Pepper).

POLICE STUFF

Fingerprints: Before fingerprinting was generally adopted in 1901 as a method of identifying criminals, police frequently used a system developed by Alphonse Bertillon, a French criminologist. The Bertillon system used the measurements of various body parts to identify and classify criminals, and was first used in America in Chicago in 1888. It has been discredited since and is no longer used.

The first fingerprint reader at the FBI was used in 1975. In 1978 the Royal Canadian Mounted Police introduced the first automated fingerprint reader.

One Adam 12: The first police car was used in Akron, Ohio, in 1899. Widespread use of cars started in the 1930s. One-way radios were introduced in Detroit in 1928. Two-way radios were not used until 1934 in Boston.

9-1-1: 9-1-1 was first introduced in 1968 by AT&T. Today, over 95 percent of the police on the street are connected to 9-1-1.

State Police: The first state police department was formed in Pennsylvania in 1905, and was modeled on the Royal Irish Constabulary. The formation of state police was often a response to the inability (or unwillingness) of local police departments to forcibly break up labor riots.

NONLETHAL WEAPONRY

THE TASER. A Taser uses compressed nitrogen gas to fire two probes up to 15 feet at a speed of 135 feet per second. When they make contact with the human body or clothing, a pulsed electrical charge is released, causing an immediate but temporary loss of neuromuscular control and any ability to perform coordinated action. The Taser has an automatic timing mechanism to apply the electrical charge on a sequence. This is usually a seven-second hit, then a break of about two seconds, then another hit and break, up to about thirty seconds. This is to keep the target's nervous system from recovering too soon.

The Taser probes don't have to penetrate the skin (the electrical discharge can jump up to two inches, including through a bulletproof vest), and the pulsing electrical charge only disturbs the signals between the brain and muscles. No deaths have been recorded from using the Taser. According to the manufacturer's specs, its electrical output will not affect a pacemaker or the heart. Modern pacemakers are designed to withstand the effects of an electrical defibrillator, which hits the patient with current many times more powerful than a Taser delivers.

Myotron Stun Gun: The Myotron stun gun is possibly the most effective stun device available today. It's small and doesn't look like much, fitting in the palm of the hand. It was designed for the FBI, and uses pulse waves to overwhelm the target's neuromuscular system. It is safe, though prolonged contact may leave two small scars.

The Myotron has a 12-volt battery and can handle up to four thousand bursts of one second or less without needing to be recharged. The power pack allows the Myotron to be fired repeatedly and for extended bursts without the need for recovery time in between applications. This makes the device very effective in situations where multiple attackers are involved.

The Muscle Man 200,000 Volt Mini Stun Baton: The stun baton has high power and extended reach, making it a favorite. The baton will deliver a shock when touched anywhere along the tip, preventing an assailant from taking it away.

Pepper Spray: Pepper spray uses the same chemicals as hot peppers (see also "Really Hot Food—The Chili Pepper," page 135). Pepper Shot, one brand, is a 10 percent spray rated at 2 million Scoville units (a means of measuring the hotness of peppers and spicy foods). Pepper spray causes intense pain, swelling of the mucous membranes and the veins in the eyes, and makes breathing difficult. These effects last twenty to thirty minutes with no permanent damage. Pepper sprays are safe, fast, effective, and easy to use. They are the top-selling product for self-defense for men and women in the world.

The quality of spray depends on the concentration of pepper. Eight percent or better is required for good effect. Alternately, check the Scoville rating: 1.5 million to 2 million is about right to meet law-enforcement grade. If there isn't a Scoville rating on the product, don't buy it. It may be dangerous or ineffective.

- **Pepper spray is legal in all fifty states, though possession and or use may be regulated or prohibited by law in some jurisdictions. In New York, you have to buy it from a licensed firearms dealer or a pharmacist (go figure), and in Massachusetts you have to have a firearms identification card.**

- **A study of nonlethal weapons showed that the Taser was successful in subduing a suspect 86 percent of the time, whereas beating the suspect with a flashlight worked 96 percent of the time; however, in the study, no suspects or officers were injured when a Taser was used, whereas with flashlights, 4 percent of officers and 80 percent of suspects were injured.**

- **Before rubber bullets were introduced for crowd control, wooden bullets were used. These were first introduced in Hong Kong in the 1960s, and were designed to be "skip-fired"— fired toward the ground at a slight angle, so they bounced into the legs of the targets. They were capable of breaking bones or killing the target and were discontinued.**

- **The Department of Energy's Lawrence Livermore Lab in California is investigating a "velocity range correction projectile launcher," a method of measuring the distance from the weapon to the target that automatically adjusts the speed of the projectile, thereby limiting the impact on the target.**

STUN GUN RESTRICTIONS

According to current checks, stun guns may not be used in the following states:

- Hawaii
- Massachusetts
- Michigan
- New Jersey
- New York
- Rhode Island
- Wisconsin

Or the following cities/counties:

- Annapolis, Maryland
- Baltimore, Maryland
- Baltimore County, Maryland
- Chicago, Illinois
- Crawford County, Iowa
- Philadelphia, Pennsylvania

Or the following countries:

- Australia
- Belgium
- Canada
- Denmark
- Hong Kong
- India
- Italy
- New Zealand
- Norway
- Sweden
- Switzerland
- United Kingdom

PRISONS AND SENTENCING

Prisons are rated as minimum security, low security, medium security, or high security. Most inmates are in the middle two categories. Only about 10 percent of all prisoners end up in the high-security facilities.

The average prison inmate is thirty-seven years old, Caucasian (60 percent), and male (only one-fourteenth of inmates are women). There's a 70 percent chance he's a U.S. citizen. About 16 percent of the prison population is Mexican nationals, followed by 3 percent Colombians and 2 percent Cubans.

In federal prisons, the most common sentence is between five and ten years, accounting for 30 percent of the population. Life sentences amount to only three out of every hundred inmates. Fifty-six percent of federal inmates are serving time for drug-related crimes, with firearms, explosives, and arson crimes making up about 9 percent combined. Immigration violations are in third place, and robbery, extortion, fraud, bribery, homicide, and sex offenses round out the rest. White collar crimes, such as embezzlement, make up less than 1 percent of the federal prison population.

WHERE ARE THEY NOW?

John Gotti: The "Dapper Don" was sentenced to life at the Federal Maximum Security Facility in Marion, Illinois, though he spent a fair amount of time at the United States Medical Center for Federal Prisoners in Springfield, Missouri, receiving treatment for throat cancer. He passed away in 2002.

Mark David Chapman: The man who shot John Lennon is an inmate with the New York State Department of Correctional Services in their Attica Correctional Facility.

David Berkowitz: The "Son of Sam" is being held at the Sullivan Correctional Facility in Fallsburg, New York, by the New York State Department of Correctional Services.

Charles Manson: Manson can be found at the California Department of Corrections Corcoran State Prison, in the Security Housing Unit (isolation). He was held at San Quentin for part of his sentence.

Theodore J. Kaczynski: The "Unabomber" is currently being held at the United States Administrative Maximum Facility in southern Colorado.

SERIAL KILLERS

Serial killers. The very term raises some uncomfortable sensations for most people, because these individuals are almost forces of nature, like tornadoes and earthquakes, in the capriciousness of their acts. Anyone can be at risk.

FBI agent Robert K. Ressler originated the term "serial killer" to describe multiple murderers who follow patterns of killing and violence, often due to psychological issues and needs, rather than for material gain.

Serial killers commonly exhibit three behaviors as children, though the presence of these things doesn't mean a child will grow up to be a killer, but they are warning signs. The conditions are bed-wetting, fire starting, and mistreatment of animals. About 60 percent of serial killers were bed-wetters past the age of twelve. Most have a fascination with fire and arson, and animal torture is another common trait. Many serial killers started out killing animals before moving on to humans.

Another sign to look for is a sense of isolation that has solidified by ages eight to twelve. Almost all serial killers were subjected to serious emotional or physical abuse during their childhood. Most have above-average intelligence, and many are near genius.

The United States is the leading producer of serial killers, and with rare exceptions the killers are Caucasian and male.

WORST OF SHOW

Not to imply for a moment that there is anything about serial killing to be celebrated, but if you had to make a list of the "best of the worst," it'd probably include the following killers:

Pedro Alonso Lopez. A native of Colombia, he was known as the "Monster of the Andes." Pedro is credited with over three hundred killings across three countries. A 1980 flash flood uncovered the first of his victims, leading to his arrest.

Jack the Ripper. The Ripper's true identity will likely never be known. He terrorized the lower classes, particularly prostitutes, in London's East End in 1888. His weapon of choice was a straight razor, scalpel, or similar instrument, and he stabbed and partially dismembered his victims.

Albert DeSalvo. Known as the "Boston Strangler," DeSalvo claimed thirteen lives between 1962 and 1964 before being captured. He was sentenced to life in prison, but was murdered while in jail.

David Berkowitz. Known as the ".44 Caliber Killer" and the "Son of Sam," Berkowitz terrorized the people of New York from mid-1976 until August of 1977. He killed six people and wounded seven. The nickname "Son of Sam" came from a note left at one murder scene that stated, "I am the Son of Sam, I am a little brat." Berkowitz believed that his neighbor's dog was a demon and ordered the killings. The neighbor's name was Sam. Berkowitz was caught as a result of his car being seen at a crime scene (and ticketed for a parking violation). He is serving a three-hundred-year sentence.

Ted Bundy. People who met Bundy claim that he was handsome, charming, and hard to resist. That may be why he was so successful. Most of his victims had a resemblance to his ex-fiancée, Leslie Holland. It appears he started his run in 1974 with Lynda Ann Healy. He was captured in 1976, but escaped in 1977. In 1979 he was recaptured again. He was executed in Florida in the electric chair in 1989. His estimated tally is between thirty and forty victims.

Jeffrey Dahmer. Dahmer was both a killer and cannibal. When police entered his apartment, they found bodies and body parts, including a head in the fridge, a box of skulls, and a kettle filled with hands and male genitals. It was noted by police that there was no food in the apartment, at which point Dahmer confessed that he had been living off the corpses. He was killed in prison by a fellow inmate using a mop handle.

Charles Manson. Perhaps it is not fair to characterize Charlie as a serial killer. At no time did he ever actually kill anyone. Instead, he sent his followers to do the killing for him. In August of 1969, Manson's followers broke into the home of director Roman Polanski and killed his pregnant wife, Sharon Tate, and four others. The murderers scrawled words on the walls, including "PIG" and "HELTER SKELTER." The next evening Leno and Rosemary LaBianca were also murdered. Manson and four of his associates were tried and sentenced to death, though this was converted to life after California abolished the death penalty.

Richard Ramirez. Known as the "Night Stalker," Ramirez killed in 1984 and 1985. His selection of victims was inconsistent, as were his methods, making him hard to profile. He broke into homes apparently indiscriminately, shooting, or stabbing men as they slept and assaulting women before strangling, stabbing, or shooting them. Children were also assaulted but left alive. Records show he killed at least fourteen people and assaulted dozens more. He was identified by one intended victim and caught outside a liquor store by an angry mob. He was found guilty of murder and other felonies in 1989 and is still on death row in San Quentin. He was married in 1996 to Doreen Lioy. At last report, the marriage has never been consummated.

SERIAL KILLER NICKNAMES AND ALIASES

Serial killers, like super heroes, need a brand name.

- The Torture Mother (Gertrude Baniszewski)
- The Alligator Man (Joe Ball)
- The Hillside Strangler (Angelo Buono)
- The Shoe-Fetish Slayer (Jerry Brudos)
- The Buttermilk Bluebeard (Alfred Cline)
- The Giggling Granny (Nannie Doss)
- Metal Fang (Nikolai Dzumagalies)
- The Werewolf of Wisteria (Albert Fish)
- Pogo the Clown, aka the Fat Man, aka the Killer Clown (John Wayne Gacy)
- The Happy Face Killer (Keith Hunter Jesperson)
- The Trash Bag Murderer (Patrick Kearney)
- The Singing Strangler (Edward Leonski)
- The Tourist from Hell (John Scripps)

LAST MEALS

It is a dearly held belief that a prisoner condemned to death is always allowed to pick his final meal, no matter what it is. This is not true. Meal choice is usually limited to the items available on the prison menu, and by rules generally enforced at the prison or in the prison system. You won't get a last cigarette in Texas, for example, because the facilities are tobacco free. Likewise, regulations prohibit alcohol. They can request anything they'd like (one inmate asked for truth, justice, and forgiveness). They just aren't necessarily going to get it.

The most popular beverages are iced tea, Coca-Cola (not Pepsi), milk, and coffee. The most popular choice for an entrée is a burger, with cheeseburgers being requested about one-quarter of the time. T-bone steak is the next favorite, followed by eggs (scrambled most often, but Denver omelets are particularly popular). French fries are the leading side dish. Vegetables are notably underrepresented or absent in most requests, and a significant number of meal requests include excessive amounts of food for a single person.

One inmate asked for:

- Two 16-ounce ribeye steaks
- One pound of turkey breast, sliced thin
- Twelve strips of bacon
- Two large hamburgers with mayo, onion, and lettuce
- Two large baked potatoes with butter, sour cream, cheese, and chives
- Four slices of cheese or one-half pound of grated cheddar cheese
- Chef's salad with blue cheese dressing
- Two ears of corn on the cob
- One pint of mint chocolate chip ice cream
- Four vanilla Cokes or Mr. Pibbs

LETHAL INJECTION

The common chemicals used in a lethal injection execution are sodium thiopental, which is a sedative that is fatal in large doses; pancuronium bromide, a muscle relaxant that causes the diaphragm and lungs to collapse; and potassium chloride, which causes the heart to stop beating. Death usually occurs within seven minutes of injection, and the cost of the drugs required is $86.08.

METHODS OF EXECUTION WORLDWIDE

Regardless of moral, religious, or ethical considerations, a lot of the world, including the United States, still believes that the ultimate punishment is in order for certain crimes. In the case of the United States, it depends on the state in question. Some, such as Texas and Florida, exercise the death penalty with relative frequency. Others do not.

The United States allows the widest variety of execution methods, including firing squads, gas chamber, lethal injection, the electric chair, and hanging. (By the by, the United States is the only country that allows the use of either the electric chair or the gas chamber.)

The firing squad is the most popular method of execution in use today outside the United States Seventy-three countries use it, forty-five of them exclusively. Hanging is second in use, with fifty-eight countries using it. Lethal injection is practiced only in a few cases, in spite of the ease with which it may be done compared to firing squads, electrocution, or hanging.

A few countries prefer a more biblical approach to the ultimate form of personal retribution. Stoning is still practiced in Afghanistan, Iran, Pakistan, Saudi Arabia, the Sudan, and the United Arab Emirates. Sudan also still uses crucifixion as an acceptable punishment. Decapitation is also in use, though only three countries—Saudi Arabia, the Congo, and the United Arab Emirates—enforce this method officially.

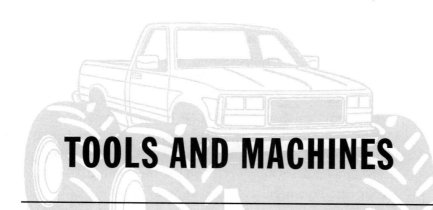

TOOLS AND MACHINES

You are a guy. Do you know where your tool box is? Better be in the back of your four-by-four . . .

Tools

ESSENTIAL TOOLS

Tools never to be without.

HAMMER: A hammer is, essentially, a lump of something hard and heavy attached to a short handle, used for striking things— nails, pegs, sheet metal, and so on. A hammer is used for the precise or imprecise and brute application of force. Hammers come in a number of varieties, weights, and intended applications. They are most commonly rated by head weight, from 6 ounces for tacking to framing hammers at 22- to 32-ounce range. (Sledgehammers are usually rated in pounds.) The standard carpentry hammer is 12 to 16 ounches. Heavier heads mean longer, heavier handles.

Hammers also get rated by the treatment of the striking face. They are either milled with a waffle head to make better contact on a nail, or bell-faced, slightly convex to drive nails without marring the wood. The striking face is generally a softer metal than the rest of the heat to avoid chipping.

SAW: Saws use a toothed metal blade used to cut metal, wood, stone, or other materials. They may be powered or manual, depending on the availability of power, the volume of work to do, the detail required, and the laziness of the user.

Saws are classified in several ways. In particular, the tooth count, measured in teeth per inch (TPI). A ripsaw has a large tooth count, typically four to seven per inch. Saws intended for finer work have higher tooth counts. The set of the teeth is the outward bend of the teeth, slightly greater than the width of the blade. A narrow blade eases the work by reducing the amount of wood to be removed. Green wood requires a greater offset to keep wet wood from clinging to the blade.

The angle of the front edge of the teeth varies as well—from a right angle to the blade to as much as 45 degrees. A right angle results in a rougher cut. A 45-degree angle is used for soft woods, and 60 degrees for hard woods.

Saws include ripsaws, crosscut saws, and panel saws. A ripsaw is used for cutting along the grain, and may have larger teeth toward the handle to maximize the cut at the most powerful part of the stroke. Crosscut saws are used for cutting across the grain. Panel saws are smaller versions of the crosscut, used for cutting thin wood or joinery.

NAIL GUNS—THE CARPENTER'S ASSAULT RIFLE: A nail gun is no substitute for a good hammer. It uses compressed air or an electric driver to rapidly force a nail—anything from tiny little finish brads to really monstrous framing nails—into wood.

They really aren't necessary for most home jobs. Nonetheless, get one. They're very cool.

DUCT TAPE: Duct tape was invented for the U.S. military as a means of keeping moisture out of cases of ammunition. The tape was composed of three layers, with polyethelyne over a fabric mesh over a rubber-based adhesive. The fabric used in the military version was cotton duck, hence the original name "duck tape."

After the war, the tape was used for sealing the seams on heating ductwork and the top-layer color was changed from olive drab to silver to make it match the sheet metal. The name was also changed to "duct tape." Technically speaking, both "duck tape" and "duct tape" are correct terms.

Duct tape can leave a residue when the tape is removed. Spraying this with WD-40 and wiping with a clean, dry cloth will remove it.

THE VICTORINOX (SWISS ARMY KNIFE): The Victorinox company was founded in Switzerland in 1884. In 1891 they delivered their first knives to the Swiss Army, establishing themselves with their most commonly known name. Today they manufacture over 120,000 per day with eight hundred different models to choose from. The largest, the Swiss Champ, has thirty-three separate features and is three and a half inches long. Television's Harry Dean Anderson made the Swiss Army knife completely cool by using one to get himself out of all kinds of jams on the show *MacGyver*.

WD-40: WD-40 is made by the WD-40 company (based in San Diego, California). The product was developed in 1953 as a material to displace water. The name means literally "water displacement formula 40," meaning that it was the fortieth try at the right mix. The formula is secret. The WD-40 company also makes 3-in-1 Oil and Lava Soap.

REAL DIMENSIONS OF LUMBER

Anyone who has gone to the lumber store to buy wood has faced the confusion of just what are those lumber dimensions all about anyway? Why isn't a two by four really two by four? And why aren't the lengths weird too?

Well, because it is that way. So deal with it. In the meantime you need to know the dimensions.

Dimension Name	Actual Dimensions
1" x 2"	¾" x 1½"
1" x 3"	¾" x 2½"
1" x 4"	¾" x 3½"
1" x 5"	¾" x 4½"
1" x 6"	¾" x 5½"
1" x 7"	¾" x 6¼"
1" x 8"	¾" x 7¼"
1" x 10"	¾" x 9¼"
1" x 12"	¾" x 11¼"
2" x 4"	1½" x 3½"
2" x 6"	1½" x 5½"
2" x 8"	1½" x 7¼"
2" x 10"	1½" x 9¼"
2" x 12"	1½" x 11¼"
3" x 6"	2½" x 5½"
4" x 4"	3½" x 3½"
4" x 6"	3½" x 5½"

BELT SANDER RACING

The National Belt Sander Racing Association (NBSRA) started in 1994 in Washington State as a result of a bet between two guys. Racing takes place between two sanders on straight track 85 feet long. The winner is the first to cross a line 50 feet down the track (the last 35 feet are for stopping). The surface of the track is rough-cut plywood, normally used for building soffits in houses. It provides good grip to the sanders and is easily replaceable.

• **Wayland the Smith was the Norse gods' craftsman.**

A sander wins regardless of how it crosses the finish line—upside down, sideways, or backward, as long as it crosses first under its own power. Races are started with a Christmas tree (a series of colored lights that warn the drivers of the start by flashing in a particular sequence), like drag racing, and jumping the starting light is grounds for disqualification.

Each sander is provided with a power cord to plug into by the NBSRA, providing 120-volt power from a 20-amp circuit.

Racing sanders are classified as follows:

3-INCH/4-INCH STOCK CLASS: As-is, out of the box with the only addition being a lane guide. The sanding belts must be off-the-shelf, at least 36 grit.

MODIFIED 3-INCH/4-INCH STOCK: Sanders may be lightened by the removal of handles or belt guards or other nonessential pieces. Modifications to the gearing and drive belts to achieve higher feet-per-minute belt speeds are also allowed. Race bodies are allowed for appearance or aerodynamics, as are lane guide modifications or additions. No belt roller modifications are allowed. The sanding belts must be off-the-shelf, at least 36 grit.

3-INCH/4-INCH   PRO-MODIFIED: Allowed modifications include stripping all excess and nonessential weight, gearing and drive belt alterations. Belts may be of any grit or belt material, stock or custom. Electrical motor alterations are allowed. No custom motors (motors not intended for use in a belt sander) are permitted. If the motor is completely replaced, it must be installed exactly as it is in factory application.

UNLIMITED: Anything goes, with the exception that the length of the sander cannot exceed 36 inches from the tip of the lane guide to the ends of traction bars.

EXHIBITION CLASS: Not a racing class. These sanders are designed for crowd appeal and entertainment, and to perform stunts such as wheelies, tug-of-war, and jumping over motorcycles.

Expert racers recommend the following for a better, faster race:

- Make sure the lane guides are not snug to the track walls, and have been lubricated with graphite, wax, or silicone.
- Be sure the belt is running straight and true.
- Use new, sharp belts. Use a coarse grit and bring extras.

REMOVE A DIGIT WITH HOUSEHOLD POWER TOOLS

The length of time required to amputate a body part, inadvertently or intentionally, depends on several factors, most critically the tool used and its power, the
quality of the blade, and body part in question.

Average power tools used by the weekend carpenter tend to have less power
and are less reliable than the professional models. Battery-powered tools
develop less torque than 120- or 240-volt models,
and the type of blade can signifi-
cantly affect the injury's extent, the
speed of the amputation, and the
recovery.

Most wood-cutting blades will tend to shred
the skin and make more ragged edges. With a
lower tooth count, they are more likely to shatter bone or leave rough ends. Saws
with higher tooth count and those used for cutting metals, tiles, or masonry will
cut faster and more cleanly.

If the cut is quick with a good blade, the average power tool (excluding drills
and such) will take a toe or finger off in less than half a second. A good table
saw, circulaw saw, or compound miter saw can remove an entire hand in less
than two seconds, but will take longer if the blade is dull or the person moves.

In the event of an amputation, accidental or otherwise, take emergency
action immediately. Address the medical needs of the injured first and foremost.
Stop the bleeding (and remember, a tourniquet is the method of last resort—
use pressure on the wound first), treat for shock, and call the proper authorities.
While that is going on, locate the loose body part, wrap it in clean gauze, and
pack it in ice. If properly cared for, and if the patient and his/her appendage are
taken to a doctor quickly enough, it may be reattached. This needs to happen in
less than six hours.

Cars, Cars, Cars . . .

ORIGINS OF FAMOUS CAR NAMES

BUICK: Named for David Buick, an inventor who built his first car in 1900.

CADILLAC: Named for Antoine Cadillac, the founder of Detroit.

CHEVROLET: Louis Chevrolet was a Swiss race car driver and engineer who built his first car in 1911.

CHRYSLER: Walter Chrysler was a locomotive mechanic who entered into car design and manufacturing in 1912.

DAIMLER: Gottlieb Daimler founded the Daimler Motor Company in 1890.

DODGE: John and Horace Dodge began producing cars in 1914.

FORD: Named for Henry Ford.

FERRARRI: Named for Enzo Ferrari, a mechanic and race car driver.

HONDA: Named for Soichiro Honda, who founded the company as a motorcycle manufacturer after the end of the Second World War.

OLDS: Named for Ransom Olds, he designed cars and developed the first gasoline-powered lawn mower.

PORSCHE: Named for Ferdinand Porsche, a designer responsible largely for engines. His work included what would later become the Volkswagen Beetle. He never designed a car that had his name on it, but his son Ferry did.

ROLLS-ROYCE: Named for Charles Rolls and Frederick Royce.

BIG MOMENTS INVOLVING CARS

1887: The Benz is introduced as the first auto produced for sale

1897: First auto insurance policy issued in Westfield, Massachusetts

1914: First electric traffic light installed in Cleveland, Ohio

1923: Powered windshield wipers introduced as standard equipment

1939: Buick introduces turn signals

1946: Power windows introduced

1954: Padded dashboards introduced

1958: Ford introduces the electric trunk release

1963: Seat belts first offered as standard equipment

1974: National speed limit of 55 mph introduced to conserve gas

1971: Ford builds first cars with experimental airbags for testing

Off-Road and Extreme

ULTIMATE FOUR-BY-FOURS

The Big Lizzie Road Train: In the early twentieth century, the Big Lizzie road train was designed for backcountry travel and work in Australia. The road train consisted of the car and two trailers. When completed, the road train was ninety-eight feet long. It had four forward gears enabling it to reach a maximum speed of two miles per hour.

- The name "Jeep" comes from the vehicle's military designation, General Purpose, shortened to "GP." The prototype was produced in forty-nine days by the American Bantam Car Company, though the actual production of the vehicles was assigned to Ford and Willys. Over 700,000 were built.

Another model of road train was designed and built by Hardy Motors in the 1930s. This road train consisted of an eight-wheeled car and two eight-wheeled trailers, and was unique in that the front and rear axles of the car steered in opposite directions, making it possible to perform a 90-degree turn through a ten-foot-wide gate.

Hardy Motors built three road trains, one going to Russia, one to Africa, and one to Australia.

Amphibious and Four-Wheel Drive: An amphibious version of the jeep was manufactured during the Second World War. After the war, an Australian by the name of Ben Carlin obtained one (a 1942 model Ford General Purpose Amphibious, serial number 1239), and fitted it out with a more hydrodynamic nose, cabin, and larger fuel tank.

In 1950 Carlin set out to circumnavigate the globe in the "Half-Safe," as he named the jeep, crossing from Halifax, Canada, to Cape Juby, Morocco, stopping in the Azores, Madeira, and the Canary Islands en route. From there, Half-Safe drove through Europe and Asia to Calcutta, India, before taking to the water again and sailing to

Burma, then driving overland through Southeast Asia. The final legs of the trip were sailings from Vietnam to Japan, then across the North Pacific to Alaska, and finally driving to Montreal, Canada.

Carlin estimated Half-Safe had covered over 9,600 miles at sea and 39,000 miles overland on the round-the-world trip. Half-safe is on display at the Guildford Grammar School in Australia.

The Ultimate 4x4: The AM General HMMWV (high-mobility multipurpose wheeled vehicle), aka the Humvee or Hummer, is arguably the most sophisticated and most heavily armed 4x4 in the world today. The design was originated in 1979, and production began in the early 1980s. About 150,000 have been manufactured for military and government use since.

A Hummer has a full-time 4x4 system optimized for off-road performance and a brake traction control system, braking a wheel when it slips, stopping the slip and transferring torque to other wheels. Hummers also can change the air pressure in their tires from firm, to allow a good ride, or soft for crossing hard edges.

Civilian models were introduced in 1991, and sell for between $80,000 and $100,000, depending on fit-out.

MONSTER TRUCKS

In the 1970s, a St. Louis construction worker, Bob Chandler, opened an auto shop specializing in four-wheel drive, largely in response to the lack of any such shop in his area. Using his own Ford F-series pickup truck as a test subject, he tried various modifications and techniques to tune and tweak the truck into something special. The truck was used for promoting the shop and started attracting imitators.

In 1981 Chandler decided to try something a little different with the truck in an attempt to stay ahead of his competition. He arranged to set a couple of junk cars out and then proceeded to drive over them in his truck. For whatever reason, the idea appealed, and a couple of months later he repeated the stunt in front of a paying audience. For all intents and purposes, that would signal the start of monster trucking.

Monster trucking is now a sophisticated blend of marketing, show business, auto racing, and wrestling, with a healthy dose of heavy-weight engineering thrown in for good measure. Major companies, including Ford, which sponsors Big Foot, invest in the sport just as they do in other areas, and it is now recognized and sanctioned by the United States Hot Rod Association (USHRA).

A typical monster truck starts with a standard off-the-lot truck. The engine is replaced with something beefier, in the range of 550 to 600 cubic inches, using alcohol/methanol instead of gasoline, burning two and a half gallons in a single 250-foot power run; the transmission is converted to match the engine and is usually air-shifted; and the frame is lightened, from as much as 16,000 pounds down to 10,000, and strengthened with tubular metal and roll cages. The original metal bodies are removed and a fiberglass shell installed, though the shell is primarily for show. Finally, the characteristic monster tires are added (see box, "Monster Truck Tires").

In terms of expense, a basic monster truck will cost around $100,000 to start. The engines add another $35,000. For professional trucks, the costs of race and support crews, travel and living expenses, repairs, and fuel add up.

Combine a 1500-hp engine with a light truck chassis and run it up on a length of level ground, and a monster truck can reach speeds of 70 to 100 mph and get itself completely off the ground. It is not unheard of for one to clear as much as a hundred feet in distance and to go as high as twenty feet above the dirt.

In addition to crushing cars and jumping, monster trucks also engage in sprint contests (usually across crushed cars) and wrestling matches, a lot like a sumo contest if sumo wrestlers weighed 10,000 pounds and were trucks. In essence, two trucks face off and try to push each other out of a ring.

Monster trucking is an exceedingly dangerous way to have fun or make a living. High power, lots of speed, engines that might be characterized as unstable, and the essential nature of the trucks—a truck rebuilt with its center of gravity grossly shifted—are a dangerous combination.

To protect against injury and fatality, monster trucks feature protective roll cages surrounding the drivers, who wear a fire suit and gloves, helmet, and neck collar, and are held in with a five-point harness. Some of the trucks have a built-in halon fire suppression system, and "kill switches." The kill switches are designed to shut the truck down completely, and there are three: one in the driver's cockpit, one in the back of the truck, and a third, remotely controlled one that is held by a race official and used to shut things down if the driver or crew isn't able to get to the other two.

> • **Monster Truck Tires:** The typical monster truck tire starts with a stock agricultural vehicle (tractor) tire, weighing 160 pounds, 43 inches wide and 66 inches in diameter. Tractor tires are generally designed for traction, not speed, and as such have a deep tread. To be most effective on a monster truck, the treads are shaved down 1.25 inches, either by hand or with a machine developed by McCord Auto Supply. The amount of rubber removed from each tire in this process is enough to make one standard truck or automobile tire.

BIG MACHINES

Rockets: The Saturn V moon rocket is the largest rocket ever built and the most powerful vehicle yet constructed. At 363 feet tall and 33 feet in diameter, the rockets weighed in at 6 million pounds loaded. The engines provided 7.7 million pounds of thrust and could propel the upper stages to a speed of seven miles per second, sending up to forty-five tons to the moon.

At one time, early in the rocket's development, the Saturn V was also intended to be used to test a nuclear rocket stage. This was called the reactor-in-flight test (RIFT), but was never built.

A larger rocket, called the Jupiter and based on the Saturn, was planned during the 1960s by NASA, but was never built.

NASA Fast Fact: When the *Apollo* spacecraft reentered the atmosphere, the heat generated would be enough to produce 86,000 kilowatts of electricity, which is enough to light the city of Los Angeles for about one hundred seconds. This same amount of energy would be enough to lift the entire population of the United States 10.75 inches off the ground.

Biggest Shovel: The largest mechanized shovel ever made is the Marion 6360 stripping shovel. It is used for strip-mining, and stands over twenty-one stories tall. One of the metal tread links in its caterpillar tracks weighs 3.5 tons.

Biggest Airplane: The world's largest working aircraft is the Russian AN-225. Howard Hughes's *Spruce Goose* was larger, but since it is debatable whether it ever flew, the honor should be conferred on the Russians. The AN-225 is 276 feet long with a wingspan of 291 feet. The maximum takeoff weight of the plane is 660 tons, allowing for a cargo capacity of 275 tons. With six engines, it can create over 50,000 pounds of thrust. On humid days, the lower pressure zone above its wings (while it's in flight) creates a cloud bank.

Biggest Train: An Australian freight train, the BHP, is used to haul iron ore and weighs 51,000 tons (not including the four engines needed to move it).

Biggest Battleship: The largest battleship ever built was the *Yamato*, built for the Imperial Japanese Navy in 1941. The craft measured 863 feet long, 127 feet wide, and weighed 70,000 tons. Its guns could fire 3,200-pound projectiles over twelve miles. It was sunk by U.S. Navy sea and air attacks during World War II while on its way to attack U.S. forces.

Monster Forklift: The biggest forklift ever built is made by Kalmar LMV, a Swedish company. The forklift can lift 88 tons (176,000 pounds).

Aircraft Carrier: The Nimitz-class nuclear aircraft carriers (classified as CVNs in navy parlance) displace approximately 97,000 tons when fully loaded, and are capable of moving at speeds in excess of 30 knots. They are 1,092 feet long, with a 252-foot-wide flight deck, and each one costs about $4.5 billion. In terms of fuel efficiency, if they ran on gasoline, they'd get about six inches to the gallon.

Supertankers: At last check, the largest supertanker in the world is the *Jahre Viking*, formerly known as the *Seawise Giant*. She measures 1,504 feet long and 226 wide, and has a capacity for over 560,000 tons of cargo.

Submarines: The Russian TK 208–class ballistic-missile subs, known to NATO as the Typhoon class, are the largest submarines ever built. Submerged, they displace 33,500 tons, and measure 562 feet long and 80.7 feet wide. They are reported to be capable of over 25 knots of speed and depths in excess of 1200 feet, and carried twenty ballistic nuclear missiles. A total of six were built, though only three are still in service. One of the unusual aspects of the sub's design was that it had twin pressure hulls inside an outer hull. Most other submarines use a single pressure hull.

GUY JOBS

There are all kinds of jobs that guys can do. Being a CPA is a job that a guy can do. So is working pulling shots at the local McCoffee. But why would a guy want to have a job like that? Any job a guy does should be either dangerous or increase his odds of pulling in the chicas—or both.

Cool Jobs

HOW TO BECOME AN ASTRONAUT

Becoming an astronaut is not easy. NASA is very picky about whom they send into space, in terms of health, skills, mental balance, and usefulness. If you're set on being the next Buzz Aldrin, there are hoops to jump through:

- Applications for NASA's Astronaut Candidate Program are accepted on an ongoing basis. One can either begin as a "pilot astronaut" or a "mission specialist astronaut" candidate.

- To even be *considered* as a mission specialist astronaut candidate, you have to have a bachelor's degree from an accredited institution in engineering, science, or mathematics, plus at least three years of professional experience. Advanced degrees are preferred.
- You also have to be able to pass a NASA Class II space physical examination, including a visual acuity of 20/20 or better without correction in both eyes. Your blood pressure must be no higher than 140/90, and your height should be between 4'10" and 6'4".
- To be considered as a pilot astronaut candidate, the same educational and work experience requirements apply. This means your visual acuity must be 20/20 or better, uncorrected, in both eyes, and your height needs to be between 5'4" and 6'4" (must have to do with reaching the pedals).

- To be a pilot, you must have logged at least one thousand hours as pilot in command in jet aircraft. Any extra experience as a test pilot will be smiled on. You must be a U.S. citizen.

NASA's problem is not finding enough qualified candidates but thinning the field. It is suggested that you have a Ph.D., specializing in something NASA needs. It doesn't hurt to be personable, a good speaker, a hard worker, and have a squeaky clean record (a security clearance is required, which means detailed and extensive background checks).

If you are tapped for consideration, you'll be interviewed, examined, and evaluated before taking up the one-year training program in Houston at the Johnson Space Center. Getting accepted and into this part of the program does not guarantee you a trip into space. You have to make it through training first, and even then you may be assigned to other duties.

- For $1 million, Russian cosmonauts unfurled an advertisement for Pepsi outside the *Mir* space station.

- If you want to go into space and you've got a bundle of money to play with, you can probably pay someone off. Start with the Russians. The Russian space agency allowed American Dennis Tito to fly on a *Soyuz* capsule to the new International Space Station in exchange for $20 million.

WHERE THE ASTRONAUTS COME FROM

According to published records, the best city to be from if you want to be an astronaut is Boston, Massachusetts, which boasts a total of nine. Chicago, Cleveland, and New York City are tied at second with eight each; however, Cleveland boasts astronauts with more missions and space time than any other city in the United States. The first men on the moon, Neil Armstrong and Edwin "Buzz" Aldrin Jr., were born in Wapakoneta, Ohio, and Montclair, New Jersey, respectively.

SMOKE JUMPER

A smoke jumper is a firefighter who parachutes into remote areas (often into rough terrain or tree-covered areas), to fight a fire hand-to-hand as it were. Once landed, often in trees or brush, the smoke-jumper must hike to the scene of the fire and begin fighting it by cutting fire lines and creating back burns (setting fires to consume fuel ahead of the fire's path).

• **Lightning causes 80 percent of all wildfires.**

The work is manual (allowing for chain-saws)—heavy equipment such as bulldozers and backhoes are brought in to fires by road where possible—and physically exhausting, with the jumpers contending with little sheep, high temperatures, and brutal terrain.

There are nine U.S. Forest Service and Bureau of Land Management regional smoke jumper bases in the western United States. When a fire is reported, jumpers are dispatched based on location, fire seize, and availability. Smaller fires can be dealt with quickly just by the jumpers, but for larger fires they work with water bombers—airplanes and helicopters that drop water mixed with retardant on the head of a fire. Supplies are also dropped from aircraft.

You must have experience in fighting fires in wilderness areas, be physically fit, able to pass annual tests, self-sufficient, and willing to engage in hard work at low pay. The job is dangerous, though from the fire and not from the parachuting. "Pancaking" (the result of a chute failing to open) happens on very rare occasions—but it does happen.

TRIPLE NICKEL SMOKE JUMPERS

The first parachute unit made up entirely of African Americans was the 555th Parachute Infantry Battalion, also known as the "Triple Nickels." Instead of being deployed in Europe to fight the Nazis, the battalion was sent to Pendleton, Oregon, assigned and trained in firefighting by the U.S. Forest Service, and became history's first military smoke jumpers.

Dangerous Jobs

DANGEROUS JOBS, DANGEROUS PLACES

Work can kill you. You need not be a mercenary in Angola (see sidebar "Other Really Dangerous Jobs"). The most dangerous jobs (fatalities per 100,000 people) according to the U.S. Department of Labor year 2000 statistics are in descending order of danger:

1. Timbercutter/lumberjack
2. Airplane pilot
3. Construction laborer
4. Truck driver (truck drivers actually had the highest number of work-related fatalities)
5. Farm laborer
6. Groundskeeper
7. General laborer (nonconstruction)
8. Police officer/detective
9. Carpenter

Based on data from 2000, the most dangerous states to work in, in terms of total number of work-related fatalities, are:

1. Texas
2. California
3. Florida
4. North Carolina
5. New York

The safest states (in 2000) were:

1. Rhode Island
2. Delaware and New Hampshire (tied)
3. Vermont
4. Hawaii
5. Maine

STACKING THE ODDS IN YOUR FAVOR

To have the minimum chance of being killed on the job, you should be:

A woman: 92 percent of workplace fatalities happen to men

Native Hawaiian or Pacific Islander: Caucasians account for 72 percent of all fatalities

Under twenty years of age: Thirty-five to forty-four years old is the most dangerous age

Self-employed: 80 percent of all people killed on the job were employed by others

MINE SWEEPER

Land mines are the worst by-product of modern warfare. Many countries around the world have large concentrations of mines left from years of warfare. According to statistics, a land mine kills or maims a person every hour of every day somewhere in the world.

Kuwait paid about $1 billion to clear seven million mines left over from the Gulf War, and typical salaries for mine removal specialists run up to $90,000 a year. Military specialists remove a lot of the mines, but there are over twenty commercial firms that provide the service. Mines are detected using specially trained dogs, electronic sensors, and visual and tactile inspection. When located by hand, a mine detection expert probes the ground at an angle, gently.

• **During the Gulf War, the Iraqis used a lot of Italian-made mines—a large percentage of which were ineffectual since they neglected to pull out the pins that would have armed them.**

• **In mine-clearing operations in Bosnia and Herzegovina between 1996 and 2000, mines were removed at an average cost of $1.59 per square meter of ground.**

Metal detectors are less commonly used with modern mines as many are composed of plastic or ceramics. A cautious nature is essential.

Mines are destroyed in place using flails (wheeled or tracked vehicles that turn or beat the ground to detonate the mines). In some cases mines are defused and removed by hand for destruction, usually by burning them.

ESTIMATED MINE DEPLOYMENT WORLDWIDE		
Country	**Average Number per Square Mile**	**Estimated Total Mines**
Bosnia-Herzegovina	152	3 million
Cambodia	142	10 million
Croatia	92	2 million
Iraq	60	10 million
Egypt	59	15 million
Afghanistan	40	10 million
Angola	31	15 million
Eritrea	28	1 million
Iran	25	16 million
Mozambique	7	2 million
Somalia	4	1 million
Ukraine	4	1 million
China	3	10 million
Sudan	1	1 million

UN PEACEKEEPER

If the idea of being simultaneously heavily armed and emasculated appeals to you or if you feel a need to die as a martyr to the cause of world peace, why not consider the role of United Nations peacekeeper?

Members of the United Nations periodically send armed troops into problem areas to separate belligerents and help cool things down. In theory, this is not unlike stepping between two fighters and pushing them apart. If they can't reach each other, they can't hit each other. In practice, instead of hitting each other, they often end up hitting the peacekeeper.

UN peacekeepers frequently consist of small forces, usually out-

numbered and outgunned. They are issued bright white
vehicles and blue helmets, making them
excellent targets. The rules that the UN places
on peacekeeping forces are intended to avoid
escalating a conflict, and this translates to
turning the other cheek. They can be in-
sulted, abused, assaulted, and shot at, but are required to get permission before they respond.

> • To help protect the environment,
> UN peacekeeping forces use only
> photodegradable sandbags.

PEACEKEEPER CASUALTIES

UN peacekeeping forces were first deployed in 1948 in the Middle East, and between then and September of 2001, the forces have had 1,709 fatalities. These break down as follows:

Hostile Acts	578
Accidents	721
Illness	296
Other	105

In the fifty-four operations undertaken, UNOC (United Nations Operations in Congo), the deployment in the Congo between 1960 and 1964, had the highest casualty rate, with 250 deaths. UNIFIL (United Nations Interim Force in Lebanon) in 1978 (the withdrawal of Israeli troops from southern Lebanon) comes in at number two with 244 deaths.

Countries with the Highest Military Casualties While on Peacekeeping Missions:

Canada	106
India	106
France	94
Ghana	94
Great Britain	90

OTHER REALLY DANGEROUS JOBS

Mercenary: Some call them "soldiers of fortune" or "mercs," but in this day and age of corporate double-speak, the favorite term for it is "outsourcing military services." To become a mercenary, it is essential to have military experience in combat conditions, and a broad knowledge of tactics and operations in small formations. Those with multiple areas of expertise (such as demolitions, languages, and communications) are more highly prized for their versatility. Veterans of elite military groups (British SAS, U.S. Army Special Forces, SEALs, Rangers, or marines, for example) are good candidates.

Oil Well Firefighter: The popular image of the oil well firefighter is John Wayne using nitro in a stream of burning oil to blow the fire out by consuming all the oxygen in the immediate area. This is wrong on two counts: first, explosives are rarely used in fighting oil well fires (being overkill), and second, the explosives do not use up the oxygen; in fact, they act in the same way as blowing out a birthday candle, by separating the fuel from the fire.

Most oil well firefighters specialize in cleaning up the wellhead, clearing extraneous debris, and then capping it with a new valve. Extinguishing the fire is a necessary first step, most often done with water and fire hoses to cool the oil to below its ignition point. The water stream also blows the column of oil emerging from the well away from the fire plume above it. If the fuel source is removed from the source of ignition, the fire is extinguished easily.

The fee per oil well is between $20,000 and $200,000, depending on the location and nature of the fire. Crews make between $300 and $1,000 a day, depending on job responsibility and experience.

Bodyguard: Being a bodyguard or executive security type is not that dangerous a job. Only a few work for celebrities and the wealthy, and as such occasionally get modest amounts of excitement; however, according to the former director of security for an American software mogul, the bodyguard should be most concerned about where the nearest hospital is in the event his employer has a heart attack. Armed attacks, kidnapping, or terrorist actions are rare, though they do happen.

For the most part, bodyguards are employed to provide a presence. The best candidates are ex-secret service, ex-police, and ex-military. South and Central America are the best job markets at the moment, and are likely to involve a higher than average rate of serious incidents due to the current spate of kidnappings in these regions. The average bodyguard makes between $200 and $300 a day.

Bounty Hunter: Bounty hunters are employed by bail bondsmen to return fugitives to court when the fugitive has failed to show for a court-mandated appearance and the bondsman is risking losing his or her bond for the individual in question. Pay depends on the fugitive and the bond amount. Most bounty hunters take 10 to 30 percent of the bond amount, but only if they are successful. A background in tracing people and law enforcement is helpful. Bounty hunters are allowed to carry firearms when licensed to do so, though some states forbid the operation of bounty hunters, armed or not, within their borders. There are an estimated 2,000 bounty hunters in the United States, and they bring in about 20,000 of the 35,000 bail jumpers each year.

New York Bike Messenger: At any given time during the business day in New York City, as many as 1,500 bike messengers are getting paid as little as $3 a trip to work the streets of the city, dodging cabs and cars. On a good day, a messenger can make $125. The faster he pedals, the more he makes, especially during rush hour. To become a bike messenger, a person needs to supply a good mountain bike (costing between $500 and $2,500), helmet and safety gear, and health insurance. A bag to carry the packages in and a communications device (walkie-talkie, cell phone, pager, or all of the above) are supplied by the company. Tattoos seem to be a requirement as well.

Cab Driver: Most cab drivers are independent contractors, renting their vehicle from a licensed cab operator. The drivers pay approximately $60 a day for car rental and gas. They receive no benefits, worker's comp, insurance, or paid holidays. Not surprisingly, the majority of cabbies are recent immigrants to the U.S. who are willing to take this low-paying and dangerous work as a means of earning some income. Cab driving is dangerous. In a five-year period in New York, 192 cabbies were killed during robberies, over an average theft amount of $100.

Cab drivers cite the best parts of their job as flexible hours and interesting people.

Central Intelligence Agency Officer: The American intelligence apparatus employs some 100,000 people in over twenty-five different agencies and organizations. Most staff falls into the category of professional positions, language experts, analytical positions, and technical/scientific positions. A very small group belong to an arm characterized by the CIA's own employment page as "Clandestine Services."

Clandestine Services and covert operations are initiated only at the direction of the president. Covert actions are called for when normal diplomatic or public channels are inadequate or inappropriate and military action is too extreme. Covert actions must be reported to the intelligence oversight committees of Congress. Check the CIA website for job descriptions.

Hostage Rescue Team Member: The Federal Bureau of Investigation's Hostage Rescue Team (HRT), based in Quantico, Virginia, is part of the Tactical Support Branch of the Critical Incident Response Group (CIRG).

There are ninety-one agents of the HRT. Any special agent may volunteer for the HRT. They must demonstrate their abilities during a two-week selection process, followed by four months of initial training for selectees. Training is ongoing and may include urban operations, mobile assault, high-risk arrests and searches, manhunt and rural operations, maritime operations, helicopter operations, and weapons of mass destruction.

The mission of the HRT is to deploy to any location in the United States within four hours of notification by the director of the FBI or his designated representative, and to conduct a successful rescue of Americans or others being held by criminals or terrorists. They may perform other law enforcement activities as directed by appropriate authorities, and operate overseas, either to rescue U.S. citizens or to support foreign operations if requested.

About the Author

Hunter S. Fulghum has never had a manicure in his life. He prefers to let the torn, callused state of his hands speak for him. He can't really talk about what he does for a living, but it involves your personal protection. When he isn't imploding football stadiums or juggling explosives, he relaxes by climbing mountains or scuba diving in the frigid waters of Alaska. He is also the author of several books, including *Don't Try This at Home* and *Like Father, Like Son*. He lives somewhere on the West Coast, and has never met Bruce Willis, but would love to go have a beer with him sometime.